THE ROGUE, PORTRAIT OF A RIVER

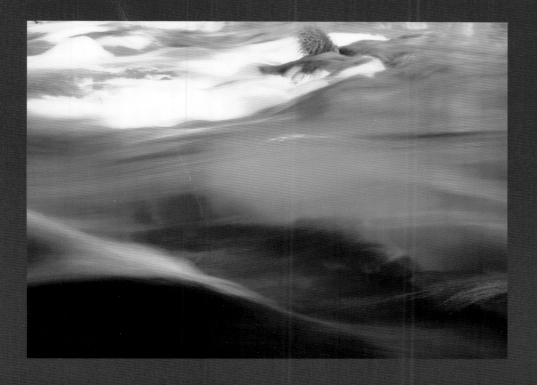

THE
ROGUE

Portrait of a River

PHOTOGRAPHS AND TEXT BY
ROGER DORBAND

FOREWORD BY JOHN KITZHABER, M.D.
QUOTATIONS FROM ZANE GREY

Raven
studios

CONTENTS

Deep and dark green, swift and clear, icy cold and as pure as the snow from which it sprang, the river had its source in the mountain under Crater Lake. It was a river at its birth; and it glided away through the Oregon forest, with hurrying momentum, as if eager to begin the long leap down through the Cascades.

—ZANE GREY

FOREWORD
by John Kitzhaber, M.D.

WHEN I WAS ASKED TO WRITE a brief foreword for this book, I was at once honored and at a loss for words. What can I possibly say that will add to what Roger Dorband has already said—through words and pictures—in this remarkable work? His prose flows easily and naturally through the story of a timeless river — touching on its history, its geology, and on the many creatures (human and otherwise) that depend on it; drawing life, livelihood, and a deeper meaning and sense of connection from its steep canyon walls and emerald water. His photographs—each a masterpiece in itself—capture what words are incapable of expressing: the spirit and the essence of the Rogue River—something intangible yet palpable; ancient yet young and new; the sense of awe and connection I feel when deep in the canyon, especially at night with brilliant stars overhead and the murmur of distant rapids in my ears.

Rivers have always held a special place in my heart, instilled, I am sure, during the many camping trips that our family took during summer vacations when I was a boy. We would sally forth, armed only with a Coleman stove (which I still use) and a huge canvas umbrella tent supported by an elaborate metal infrastructure which could attract lightning strikes from miles away. We camped on the shores of Bear Lake, Utah, in the Snowy Range of Wyoming, and on the banks of rivers—the Snake and Clearwater in Idaho, the South Platte in Colorado, and the Hoh on the Olympic Peninsula of Washington.

As I grew older, my father and I left the umbrella tent behind and took our stove to the banks of the great rivers of western Oregon—rivers with names like Santiam, Umpqua, and Rogue. It was along these rivers that I first met the salmon in its native habitat and developed my life-long fascination with it and its life cycle. It was here that I first watched wild Chinook fight their way upstream against the current—leaping impossible falls, hurtling their silver bodies skyward with the spray breaking the light into rainbows.

If I had to pick a metaphor for the Rogue River, something that captures its essence—the intangible dimensions of this special place — it would be the life cycle of the salmon which is, more than anything else, dedicated to the future—to nurturing, sustaining, and giving to that which will follow. The salmon I grew to know when I was a boy were born in the gravel beds of the cold, fast-moving streams that tumble down the west slope of the Cascade Mountains. They migrate down these rivers to the ocean, where they mature and spend their adult lives until some inner voice tells them it is time to come home.

On its final journey, this remarkable creature travels thousands of miles through a gauntlet of predators—struggling up swift emerald rivers, leaping falls, and negotiating obstacles—in a single-minded effort to return to the very gravel where it was born. Those few that arrive safely then spawn and leave their eggs buried in the gravel to hatch, to migrate to the sea, to grow to maturity, and to return—continuing the cycle. But even those that never spawn—those that die in the attempt — give their bodies to the river and to the future, providing the nutrients essential to the survival of the next generation.

That, to me, is the Rogue River—at least the one I have known—the heart of an endless cycle as old as the universe and as young as the mist chased up the canyon walls by the morning sun: a flashing silver body in the roar of Rainie Falls; a spent salmon floating on its side in the deep current below Horseshoe Bend, gently giving itself back to the river; the naked challenge of Blossom Bar; the elemental power of the Coffee Pot in Mule Creek Canyon; an osprey cutting the water like a knife and rising into the soft evening air with a shivering silver trout in its talons; vultures keeping their patient watch in the calm between Wildcat and Tyee; an otter at Marial; an eddy at Whisky Creek; a bear in camp; wood smoke at dawn; the scream of a bald eagle echoing down the walls of Dulog Canyon.

This is the Rogue I have known and rowed and loved. My son Logan has yet to experience its magic and its wonder; he has yet to unlock its secrets and to learn its lessons. But one day soon he will drop through Upper Grave Creek Falls and into the canyon. And when he emerges three or four days later at Foster Bar, he will be changed forever.

That is why it is important to read this book—to savor the words and to lose ourselves in the majesty of the photographs. For only by experiencing the Rogue River can we truly know it. And only by knowing it can we find the wisdom and the courage to honor it and to preserve it for all those who will follow. And only then can we fully appreciate our true role in the endless cycle on this glorious planet in a magnificent universe.

INTRODUCTION

Hayes Eddy

Walker Bar

A RIVER IS A LIVING THING

IN THE PACIFIC NORTHWEST, rivers flow through our lives with an energy and constancy as persistent as time itself. No two are the same, yet each shapes the life and land around it as surely as snow melts and water runs downhill. This book is a celebration in photographs and words of southern Oregon's Rogue River, which has been shaping my life for over 60 years.

When I think river, I am thinking Rogue. It is the first and the last, the one that flows through my dreams and imagination. I spent my early, most impressionable years growing up in the Rogue Valley. Since I left there in 1962 to attend college, the valley has not been my place of residence. Nonetheless, I have returned many times to visit family and friends, and always to reconnect with the river.

Getting to know a river can be a lifelong journey. Like the ever-changing background of an epic story, in my life the Rogue has been a place to gather with others, a fortress of solitude, an aid to memory, a song, a quality of light, a cradle of dreams, a resting place, a source of energy, a giver of joy, and a receptacle of sorrow. At times, it has been a perfume, a stink, an ease, an obstacle, and always the living heart of the valley.

In getting to know the Rogue, I hiked every foot of designated trail along its shore. In the seven years of photographing for this book, much of the time I was following my own footprints. I believe that I boated all of the Rogue's waters that can be considered navigable, and drove, repeatedly, all the highways and secondary roads that touch it. In order to see sections of the river kept from view by private property, I confess to ignoring "no trespassing" signs and crawling underneath barb wire fences. It has been my joy over the years to wade the riffles, shoot the rapids, drift the still waters, and sit mesmerized for hours on the banks of the Rogue.

The Rogue was one of the original eight rivers in the United States to receive protection under the landmark Wild and Scenic Rivers Act of 1968. This official designation is meaningful and adds to the reputation of a river long known for its fishing, scenic beauty, and white-water rafting. All else being equal, however, it is the literature and lore of a river that sets it apart from others and piques our interest. Would the Mississippi capture our imaginations so fully were it not for the adventures of Mark Twain's Huckleberry Finn and Tom Sawyer? Would the Columbia roll on so gracefully in our mind without the lyrics of Woody Guthrie?

To date, the Rogue has been celebrated more in words than in images. Attention to the river became international in 1929 with the publication of *Rogue River Feud*, a novel by famous writer and world-class fisherman Zane Grey. Grey also wrote voluminously about the Rogue for magazines and devoted several chapters to it in *Tales of Freshwater Fishing*. Since Grey's time, there has been a steady stream of writing about the Rogue.

The spectrum of this writing is broad, including such diverse works as *Reading Appollinaire by the Rogue River* by beat poet Lawrence Ferlinghetti and *Tall Tales From Rogue River*, historian Stephen Dow Beckham's volume of collected stories by lower Rogue denizen and mail carrier Hathaway Jones. Beckham has also contributed the definitive volume on the fate of the Rogue River Natives, entitled *Requiem for a People*. Other classics of the Rogue include Kay Atwood's *Illahe*, a history of the Rogue River Canyon enriched by interviews with many descendants of the early settlers there, and Florence Arman's *A River to Run*, the colorful biography of the ultimate river man, Glen Wooldridge. Of note recently, Robin Carey, writer and fisherman, has given us *North Bank*, a memoir of the lower Rogue woven with the issues and intricacies of place gleaned through the antennae of his fly rod, and the poet and essayist John Daniel has written *Rogue River Journal*, his meditation on self and solitude during four months alone in the Rogue River Canyon.

Though not intended to be comprehensive, the text that follows gives readers the history of the Rogue River, as well as glimpses into my own personal history and that of Zane Grey. In creating the text, I have relied on many sources. I am particularly indebted to Beckham, whose work provided a framework for the compelling story of the first people living on the Rogue. In addition to the sprinkling of quotations from Zane Grey that accompany *The Photographic Journey* section of the book, I have also summoned the voices of some of my favorite writers and poets and that of a Lakota shaman, mainly to strike a tone at the beginning of a passage. I owe a large measure of gratitude to them and to the other writers and storytellers listed in the *Written Sources*. Like many of them, my main inspiration has been the ever-changing splendor of the river itself.

Below Blossom Bar

Wallace Stegner, the great writer about the American West, exclaimed, "We may love a place and still be dangerous to it." I recognize the danger in having made a book like this. I am somewhat comforted by the fact that the Rogue is not an undiscovered paradise. So I say guardedly that I hope my efforts will encourage others to become more acquainted with the Rogue, or with their own river, the one that's nearby. Too often, like a blood relative so close we can't see where our life ends and theirs begins, we tend to lose sight of our vital connection to rivers. They are a wellspring and a lifeline for all living things. I believe that a river's bounty quenches not only the body's thirst, but the soul's as well. The same may be true for other species. If we knew the soul stories of the kingfisher, the blacktailed deer, the salmon, or the salamander, we might find a meaning and poetry as rich as that of humankind, which has sung a river song throughout the ages.

Like the Rogue, a river may change its course many times, hide itself underground during a series of drought years, be dammed, dynamited, bulldozed, channeled, and piped miles from its natural bed. Still it persists, expressing a power that is the very essence of life. In celebrating the Rogue, I urge us all to preserve and protect rivers everywhere, always mindful that a river is a living thing.

Below Milk Maid Riffle

Caveman Bridge

Gilbert Creek 1948

OH GIVE ME A HOME

THERE ARE RESIDENTS of the Rogue Valley who can trace their ancestry back four or five generations to pioneer kin coming out on the Applegate Trail, hell bent on a new life. Other families in the valley speak of an early renegade forefather hiking in from the gold fields of northern California to try to strike it rich on the Rogue. My family heritage is neither of these. The history of our family on the Rogue began in 1939, just five years before I was born.

While serving in the South Seas between the World Wars, my father read of the fabulous sport fishing on the Rogue in the writings of Zane Grey. Nurturing dreams engendered by Grey, he decided to retire to southern Oregon in 1939. A city boy from Chicago, world weary from 20 years in the Navy, Al moved to the Rogue Valley for three things: the mild climate, the simple life, and the fishing.

My parents purchased and cleared a small parcel of land a few miles downriver from Grants Pass. On the pine-covered south bank above Weston Riffle, they built a modest cabin. My mother, Alice, a farm girl from Wisconsin, was no stranger to hard work. Side by side, in true pioneer fashion, she and Al finished their place in a summer and settled in. When the cabin was finished and there was plenty of wood in for the winter, Alice began planning a garden, and Al started fishing.

In accordance with the philosophy of Zane Grey, Al believed that fly-fishing was the only sportsmanlike way to take a steelhead. It required dis-

Al Dorband 1938

cernment, finesse, skill, and the ability to read the water. To hear him tell it, there was a kind of truth and integrity to fly-fishing, a Zen-like quality if you will. There was etiquette, too, proper behavior for those who practiced the art. For instance, a fly fisherman would never think of beginning downstream from a fellow fly fisherman already working a riffle. That would interrupt his progression, a serious breach. Unlike golf, there was no "playing through" either, no matter how plodding the fellow was. Above all, the true sportsman was patient, never failing to honor the sanctity and timelessness of the hours spent with a fly rod in hand.

My mother learned the rudiments of fly-fishing from Al in the lakes of the high Sierras early in their marriage. Family photographs attest to her looking the part, if not actually succeeding in catching fish. But the sport didn't take with her. She loved the Rogue more for its beauty. Alice went to the river without an agenda, purely to enjoy. Though not a naturalist in the strict sense of the word, she loved observing the flora and fauna and the seasonal changes along the river, propensities that were passed on to her children.

Late in the fall of 1941, my parents' life on the Rogue was abruptly interrupted. At the end of the full autumn season that brought the birth of my sister, Jean, and the wonderful fishing Al had enjoyed, the Japanese attacked Pearl Harbor and Al was called back into the service. As an experienced naval chief with a specialty in electronic communications, he was assigned to monitor sonar buoys in Puget Sound off of Port Townsend. Alice was able to accompany him, and it was there that I was conceived a little over a year later.

When Al's duty ended, my parents went to visit relatives in Evanston, Illinois, where I was born in May of 1944. By winter that year, we were in southern Oregon again where my parents tried to reconnect with the sweetness of their former life. Before we left Evanston, my grandmother had instructed the folks to put a little whiskey in my formula to prevent colic. I've always said that the cross-country trip at the age of six months accounts for my love of travel and taste for good whiskey. It was also that side trip to Illinois that kept me from being a true native son of Oregon, a claim I've made anyway, since I have no memories of Illinois and had no part in the decision to go there.

For the first seven years back in the Rogue Valley, our family lived in a small, white house nestled with three other modest houses at the end of Oak Street in Grants Pass. To call Oak a street at that time suggested a vision of the future on the part of municipal planners. It was a gravel road with no curbs, sidewalks, or other amenities. I could always see the cloud of dust rising from the end of the street before I spotted my father's truck when he arrived home from work in the late afternoon.

On two sides of the neighborhood were large vacant fields of indigenous grasses, weeds, and blackberry. At one time, these fields must have been used for grazing livestock, but had been allowed to go to seed, perhaps as the result of someone's development plans gone belly up. During our tenure there, they acted as a buffer from the town and its surrounding residential community, giving our neighborhood a sheltered, insular feeling.

LEFT: *Jean and Roger Dorband 1950*
BELOW: *Alice Dorband 1938*

The wooded east side of the neighborhood was bounded by Gilbert Creek, which delineated the back portion of our property. It underscored the sense of protective boundaries around the neighborhood in the way a moat protects a castle. The south side of the moat was the most impenetrable boundary of all, the river.

Our place felt rural in spite of being in the city limits. I'm sure our raising chickens, and for a short while having a kennel for springer spaniels, contributed to that atmosphere. We were part of the domesticity of a small town, while touching something wild in the form of Gilbert Creek and the river. Returning to the old neighborhood over the years, I have always felt a presence there, distinct and yet inseparable from the memories of childhood. Some of that feeling may have been the residue of what had taken place there before our time. While researching for this book, I was surprised and pleased to find out that the site of our neighborhood was an encampment of long standing for Dagelma Indians.

Geographically, our stretch of the Rogue was roughly in the middle of the river's 215-mile course from the headwaters down to the Pacific. From our house, we had to walk about 50 yards to the property of a neighbor in

Lathrop Boat Landing 1996

order to see the river. The backyard of Captain John White, a veteran of World War I, and his wife, Liberta, provided a relatively broad view of the Rogue from Riverside Park, just beyond the graceful arches of the Caveman Bridge, downriver to Tussing Riffle, a distance of about half a mile. This high embankment on the river's north side was largely covered by thick blackberry and poison oak, crested up on the flat by broadleaf maple, tan oak, Douglas fir, and the two massive old red oaks that were the corner-stones of Captain White's immaculately kept yard. Beside the view it afforded, the embankment was also our flood insurance.

Floods on the Rogue were a real danger prior to the building of Lost Creek Dam in 1978. I can remember lying in bed as a small boy, with vivid images in my mind from earlier in the day of uprooted trees bobbing in the great brown, moving mass of the flooding river that also carried a plunder of people's houses getting flushed downstream: the front porch and siding, the picket fence, along with old tires, refrigerators, clothing, anything that floated. Lying there, I would listen to the roar of the river, wondering if that night it might rise clear up to Captain White's place, take out the two mas-sive old oaks, and flood our neighborhood.

Until I was seven and able to swim pretty well, I wasn't allowed to take the trail down to the river by myself. I had the run of the neighborhood, though, and because the river was the river, a great mystery, alive, beautiful in all seasons, and dangerous too, I went to look at it often. Sometimes on the weekends when my father was off work, I would walk with him over to our vantage point at Captain White's to have "a look-see at the river," as Dad was fond of saying. He always checked the color and the clarity of the water before making a decision whether to go fishing that day. Even though skies were clear where we were, there might have been thundershowers over in Sam's Valley or up around Prospect or Shady Cove, leaving the river too murky for good fly-fishing.

Though we couldn't see the river from our house, we could smell it. What we detected may not always have been the odor of the water itself, though it certainly does have a fresher, sweeter scent in spring, gradually becoming more fecund as the season ripens, turning acrid and earthy-smelling in late fall and winter. The smell of the river, and all that it engen-dered, created the background of our lives.

The Rogue's waters provided the irrigation that sustained the fruit trees—pear, apple, cherry and peach—that brought the delicate scent of blossoms in spring. The same water wetted the hop vines in the hundreds of acres grown in those years along Upper River Road, producing the sweet-and-sour smell wafting through the valley with the harvest in September. Earlier in summer, we could smell the hay being cut in the fields on the flanks of the valley and the light essence of sawdust smoldering in the wigwam burners of the sawmills. The trail to the river was perfumed with the aroma of anise and blackberries ripening.

There were unpleasant smells as well. By mid-summer, dead spring-run salmon, their cycle completed, lay putrefying in the shallows below Gilbert

Coco 1950

Creek. At times, this horrible smell would come right into our house courtesy of our springer spaniel, Coco. During the season when the spawned-out salmon littered the riverbank, we kept him in a fenced section of the yard. Only the smell of a bitch in estrus or rotten salmon could inspire him to dig for hours in intense summer heat to get under that fence. Once free, he made a beeline for the river, where he rolled on the first salmon carcass he found before returning home proudly, as though he'd just had a bath and put on his Sunday finest. The reception my parents gave him was anything but cordial. First came incarceration, followed by a saltwater cocktail to make him vomit in the event that he had eaten any of the dead salmon, which can be fatal to dogs. After that came the ultimate humiliation, a real bath, with strong soap, lots of it, which Coco had to endure out on the lawn standing in the round, tin tub that served as a wading pool for my sister and me when we were small.

Neither of my parents were swimmers like our next-door neighbors and dear friends, Frank and Sonia Lavsky. I mention them by name because they were like second parents to my sister and me. By the time we were old enough to hike the trail down Gilbert Creek to the river, Uncle Frank and Aunt Sonia began teaching us to jellyfish float and dog paddle in the swimming hole where Gilbert Creek formed a sand bar on the edge of the Rogue.

As I was walking that same trail recently, the smell of the anise and blackberry brought on a torrent of childhood memories. I plucked a section of joint grass and put it between my lips, remembering how as children, when the joint grass was taller than we were, we pretended that the slender green sections were cigarettes.

The Lavskys introduced my sister and me to picking blackberries, too. Carrying two-pound Folgers coffee cans strung with twine hanging from our shoulders, we waded up Gilbert Creek in soggy sneakers, searching out the shady places where the largest berries hung like grapes in heavy bunches over the creek. Without saying a word, Frank and Sonia would always drop a few handfuls of berries into our buckets to make sure they were brimming when it was time to head home.

Except for regular Saturday night outings to see a movie at the Rogue Theater downtown, our family tended to stay close to home during those years. Holidays like the Fourth of July were neighborhood events celebrated with lots of festivity on the bank of Gilbert Creek, where Frank and Sonia had created a beautiful picnic area. About the only other exception to our stay-at-home lifestyle was Sunday church followed by a drive in the family conveyance, a 1942 Plymouth coupe, usually with Coco aboard as mascot.

In the late forties and early fifties, before there was a local television station, the Sunday afternoon drive was still a ritual for many families in southern Oregon. Savage Rapids Dam was one of our favorite destinations. Here the river drops 60 feet onto boulders and bedrock in an angry explosion, then storms away. For us, there was something mesmerizing in this thundering spectacle that made the world seem a calmer place away from its roar.

The real show at the dam came in the spring when the still relatively large runs of Chinook salmon came upriver to spawn. Before locating the fish ladder, the great fish would make leap after leap up the spillway. Shooting like torpedoes out of the maelstrom below the dam, they launched them-selves skyward, tails flailing wildly, only to tumble haplessly back into the froth and chaos. At the peak of the run, there would be two or three fish in the air at all times. My sister and I fervently hoped that we would see one make it over the dam, but, of course, we never did. Instead, we left for home a little disappointed and uneasy, wondering if all the salmon would find the fish ladder and their way home, too.

Gilbert Creek

Toward the end of the summer that I turned seven years old, our family left Gilbert Creek. My father's work as an electrician had become irregular in the slow economy that prevailed at that time, so we moved to Bremerton, Washington, where he could get work in the naval shipyards. Accustomed to the competitive pace of the private sector, Al found himself at odds with the lax attitude toward work in the shipyards. After a little more than a year, he terminated his employment there. Our family then moved to Pensacola, Florida, where Al imagined going into the commercial fishing business on the Gulf of Mexico with his nephew, who had a boat. But the climate in August when we arrived there, and the culture shock, were too much. By mid-September, we were back in the Rogue Valley.

Of the many motels along Highway 199 on the south side of Grants Pass, my parents chose to stay at the Flamingo, perhaps a nostalgic acknowledgment of the life they had imagined in Florida. Their lost dream notwithstanding, within two months they had reconnected with friends and rejoined the Presbyterian Church congregation. Realizing that they had come back to their true home, they bought a brand-new house on Marion Lane, somewhat removed but directly across the river from the old place on Gilbert Creek.

The new place, which was part of a small development, sat cheek to jowl with another practically its twin and only 15 feet away. I can still remember my sadness about having another house so close. More disconcerting was the fact that the river, which held a great magnetism for me, was nearly half a mile away.

Our small, ranch-style house sat on a completely flat, barren-looking lot that my parents began landscaping right away. My father turned over the thin layer of humus with his gas-powered Merry Tiller, raising stone after stone from beneath the ground. The stones were mostly smooth, rounded, and gray. River rocks! At first, there was something thrilling in the realization that although the Rogue was some distance away and close to 100 feet below in elevation, it had once flowed where our new house stood. This thrill quickly passed with the slow, laborious process of hauling rocks out and hauling dirt in, which went on for years. At times, I felt like I was chained to a wheelbarrow, and our former life on Gilbert Creek seemed all the more idyllic.

Somehow, in spite of yard work and school, I still found time to escape to the river. My bicycle became my best friend. In summer, my pals and I, dressed in our cutoffs and sneakers, would ride down to Tussing Park with our fishing poles or upriver to Riverside Park, where we hid our bikes and floated downstream on inner tubes. We sometimes let the current carry us several miles before making the long, hot return walk in the event that we couldn't bum a ride.

By the time I was a teenager, I was accessing an ever-expanding stretch of the river, still on my bicycle until I turned 16 and was occasionally allowed to use the family car. These were the years of initiation. Swimming across the river and back was a milestone for any boy or girl living along the Rogue, as was catching your first steelhead or mustering the courage to dive off the old railroad bridge, a plunge of about 40 feet.

The railroad bridge was about a mile upriver from Grants Pass. It was a hangout for teenagers, who gathered there to get away from the disapproving eyes of adults. Swimming, sunbathing, or daring each other to dive from the bridge weren't the only goings-on. There were cigarettes, beer, and transistor radios blaring rock and roll. The look of the girls' bodies in their short shorts and bathing suits made a stunning impression on me. These were heady times, when the sweet scent of Coppertone suntan oil blended with the fecund smell of the green river as it bore silent witness to our rites of passage.

Schroder Park

ABOVE: *Near Casey Park*
BELOW: *Ginger Rogers**

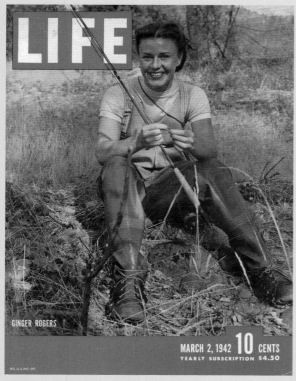

* Indicates an entry on the copyright page

The only persistent regret I had during my years of growing up in the Rogue Valley was that our family never boated on the river. Looking back, I'm sure the reason was primarily that Al and Alice didn't swim. The boating options were narrower then, too. Rafting did not become a popular activity on the Rogue until years after I had graduated from high school, and jetboat excursions were not yet available. The only viable means of being on the river was a wooden driftboat used primarily for fishing.

Often while bank-fishing for long hours, my father and I would witness a driftboat silently floating by like a mirage. In those moments, I felt tremendous envy, especially if we weren't catching anything. Usually, a guide would be at the oars, hosting a couple of "dudes" and telling them where and when to fish. Being the witness to what I imagined was their privileged life stung. What stung more was the sense that I was just observing a life of adventure that others were living. On the other hand, when talk would turn to the celebrities who frequented the river, our lives seemed lifted momentarily above the mundane.

Among the legions of those who came there were many who seemed larger than life: Winston Churchill, President Hoover, General Curtis LeMay, the writer Jack London, and sports heroes Babe Ruth and Ted Williams. Clark Gable, an avid fisherman, became a denizen of the Rogue. He often brought buddies like Bing Crosby along from Hollywood. The actress Ginger Rogers, who was highly skilled with a fly rod, bought a large ranch on the upper Rogue in 1940. Her fishing exploits on the river were written up in *Life* magazine, whose cover featured a picture of her in waders, holding her fly rod. No one I ever met claimed to have seen any of the celebrities in the flesh, but practically everyone knew someone who thought they had. The word was that you wouldn't recognize most of these folks without their makeup.

Whenever celebrities came up in conversation, I felt restless. Unlike my father, whose dreams brought him to the Rogue Valley in search of a peaceful life away from the city and military life, I dreamt of being elsewhere, away from what I perceived as the humdrum of small-town life. I eventually left the Rogue Valley, pursuing a life of art and travel, while Al seemed to find contentment there. Even after the best fishing years had passed and he would frequently return from the river with an empty creel, fishing represented the active pursuit of his dream. Zane Grey once claimed it was the connection with nature that mattered most to him, not whether he caught a fish. Al, too, revered nature, but I believe of equal importance to him was a sense of belonging. Just as he found camaraderie in the Navy and later as a member of the Order of Masons, on the river he saw himself as a member of a great fraternity of sport fishermen, with Zane Grey as its ex officio president. They were sportsmen in the true sense of the word, men who upheld fly-fishing as a way of life. Theirs was a brotherhood of hope, waxing and waning in the long hours while they waited for a big one to bite. Hope, that most underrated emotion, giving meaning and poignancy to their lives.

Though my sister and I have lived away from the Rogue now for many years, we both have an abiding notion of buying land along the river and returning some day in our retirement. Given the current trend in the price of real estate in the Rogue Valley, the possibility now seems pretty remote. Still, the river runs deep in our family. Al and Alice continued to live on Marion Lane the rest of their lives. Al spent his last night there 24 years from the time he bought the property. He was 72 years old. Alice died in her bed there in 1995 at the age of 83. Both of our parents are buried at the Memorial Gardens, which lies in the Rogue's floodplain less than a mile from the river's shore and not far from their first cabin.

When I don't have time to visit the Rogue, I often travel on it or have adventures along its banks in my dreams. I have saved both of my parents from drowning in the Rogue, taken Rainie Falls in a puny wooden rowboat, exhumed the bones of cavalrymen killed by Indians at Galice Creek, struck it rich panning for gold, and met an old Eskimo shaman, all in dreams. Dreams of my father are almost always set along the Rogue. Shortly after Dad died in 1976, my sister Jean, who lives in Germany, saw him in a dream. Suffused in the mild, late-afternoon light, he stood waist deep in the river at Finley Bend, a favorite outing place for our family. Smiling slightly, he slowly turned away, bent forward, let himself slip beneath the dark water, and was gone.

Finley Bend

FAR LEFT: *Zane Grey 1936**
ABOVE: *Zane Grey's cabin*

ZANE GREY AND THE ROGUE

THERE IS SOMETHING MEMORABLE in the name Zane Grey. Once heard, it is seldom forgotten, just like the name of the southern Oregon river that he loved. Zane Grey and the Rogue River are forever linked.

During Grey's lifetime, his name was a household word. By 1910, he was well known and making a good living as a Western writer. In 1912, at the age of 40, he published *Riders of the Purple Sage,* his most famous novel. It sold more than a million copies and established Grey as the most popular and highest-paid writer in America, a distinction he held for 20 years. Though he had some relatively lean years, particularly during the Great Depression, money was no longer an issue for Grey after 1912. From that time forward, he wrote and spent the proceeds freely, primarily on fishing.

I first heard Zane Grey's name in the fishing stories my father told. Ordinarily a laconic and modest man, Al would drop Grey's name on occasion when some braggadocio with a spinning rod and his first steelhead cast a derisive remark about the fly rod that was Al's standard.

Typically, the neophyte, commonly referred to as a "dude" in the parlance of the guides and experienced fishermen on the Rogue, would walk up conspicuously displaying his catch before launching into a soliloquy about his heroic effort landing the fish. Al's poker face and his unswerving attention to his own business would frustrate the man's efforts at self-aggrandizement, resulting in a sideways glance at Dad's fly rod followed by the condescending, "Doin' any good with that thing?"

If Al was in the mood and decided the dude needed some schooling, he began with a dispassionate appraisal of the fellow's catch, followed by the comment that the fishing was nothing compared to the way it had been in the early forties. If he caught the fellow's attention, Dad would then recount in matter-of-fact language how, while in the Navy, he had read of the Rogue's fantastic steelhead fishing and beautiful scenery in the writing of the famous fisherman Zane Grey. "When I retired from the Navy in '39, I came here for the fishing," Al went on. "Now, I guess I stay because of the weather."

Borrowing a word favored by Grey, Al proceeded to tell about the steelhead fishing during the "glory" years of the forties when no real sportsman used anything but fly-fishing gear. During that period, he often caught a limit of steelhead before breakfast. The abundance kept his smokehouse going from early September until the end of fall. In October of 1941, the run of steelhead was so bountiful that Al hooked a fish on the first cast for a period of two weeks straight. This portion of Dad's dissertation was his *pièce de résistance*, not proffered until he was sure the dude was well hooked and listening respectfully. Though it sounded like a fabrication, particularly in light of the sorry state of the fishing during the fifties, it was not. The proof existed in the form of a small notebook Al always kept to record the day's events, a practice he had developed as a chief petty officer in the Navy.

The "glory" years were over by the time I was born, but I lived them vicariously through Al's stories, which I frequently recounted to my friends in great detail, down to the royal coachman fly, which was his favorite. When I wanted to impress a new kid in the neighborhood, I would lead him to the old smokehouse at the back of our property. Though it was just a dilapidated shack that had not seen significant use for a number of years, the smokehouse was the perfect setting for my endeavor. The old siding, saturated with the sweet, spicy essence of hickory, salmon, and steelhead, gave off a wonderful aroma. There in the semidarkness, sitting Indian fashion on the rough plank floor, I could feel the nostalgic aura of the "glory" years sweeping over us.

The main purpose of these sessions was to convince the listener that I was part of a long lineage of great fishermen. Regardless of which of my dad's fishing stories I was about to tell, I began by conjuring the names of famous fishing guides and river men on the Rogue, men like Glen Wooldridge, who was still alive at that time and had guided Zane Grey on several fishing trips. Grey, of course, was given a special status, the founder of fly-fishing on the Rogue, the granddaddy of us all.

At that time, I had not read Zane Grey and knew very little about him. I knew he had built a cabin somewhere far downriver, where he had written a book about the Rogue. I also knew that this book and his other writing brought many other famous people to fish the Rogue. It was the fame and celebrity associated with Zane Grey that made him mythological in my estimation. A man who wrote and fished and was famous. And somehow Al and his fly rod and his son were connected with this man. We who lived modestly and had to work hard for a living, as most did in the Rogue Valley in those years, once had among us a man who was different.

In the vernacular of the fisherman, the phrase "wetting a line" has obvious meaning. For a few anglers who carry pen and notebook, putting down lines of language when the fish are not biting or by campfire light at the end of the day, the phrase has double meaning.

There are numerous parallels in the dual activities of the writer-fisherman. In order to succeed, an early rise is best. Persistence and great patience are needed, as are a cool head and a steady hand to counter the excitement of line peeling out when a big one is on. A philosophical bent in the face of waxing and waning hope also serves the writer-fisherman well. Above all, to be a great writer or fisherman, one must have passion, and doubly so for someone who is both. Such a passionate man was Zane Grey.

Casey Park

Whether the quest was for tuna off the coast of Nova Scotia, marlin in the tropical waters of Tahiti, or steelhead on the Rogue River, Zane Grey pursued his twin passions with gusto and flair. He traveled extensively, often accompanied by an entourage of friends, fishing buddies, cameramen and photographers, secretaries and, occasionally, family. It was not just his talent and enthusiasm that set Grey apart from the mainstream, but a combination of self-promotion and an unerring ability to create his own celebrity, amplified by a penchant for extravagance. He often fished where others had not, and he never shied away from adventure.

A classic example was his 1925 driftboat expedition down the Rogue from the head of what is now the Wild and Scenic section of the river down to the Pacific, a distance of about 100 miles. Very few had undertaken this feat, which was considered extremely hazardous at the time. Grey's party accomplished this before many of the most difficult rapids had been cleared of dangerous boulders by dynamiting in the following two decades. For the most part, Grey rowed his own boat, one of several that were made especially for him for his downriver trip. They were skiffs actually, a narrower and lighter version of the driftboats used today, made solely of wood and without the benefit of the fiberglass and steel incorporated in some of the modern boats.

In *Rogue River Feud*, written in 1927 while living in his cabin at Winkle Bar, Grey draws heavily on the memory of this downriver journey. A claim can be made that the guide on that trip, a fellow named Claud Barton, was the prototype for the protagonist in the book. The book demonstrates how well Grey knew the places and the people he wrote about. The characterizations and descriptive accuracy of his novels have fostered a rediscovery of his work among historians and scholars. Justifiably, his son, Dr. Loren Grey, recently wrote that his father "played a major role in defining America's perception of the West and indeed, of ourselves, as well."

Throughout the twenties Grey continued to travel and fish in the Galapagos, Nova Scotia, Tahiti, and New Zealand. Between these saltwater expeditions, he frequented the Rogue. Ostensibly, it was the fishing that kept drawing Grey back to the Rogue Valley. But there was more to his returning than just catching a fish. He was captured by the beauty, the climate, and the sense of peace he felt there. Expressing the rapture he felt in nature, Grey wrote, "Personally whether I catch a bass or trout or no fish at all is a small matter." What a revelation coming from arguably the most avid fisherman of his era! The true motivation behind Grey's endless expeditions and torrent of words was his love of nature itself. In nature, he felt the same exultation and mystical awe experienced by Henry David Thoreau and the English poet William Wordsworth, both of whom Grey read throughout his life.

Though, paradoxically, he considered himself unlucky as a fisherman, Zane Grey's accomplishments in the sport were legendary in his day. During his lifetime, he held 16 all-tackle deep-sea world records for such species as the bluefin and yellowfin tuna, the blue marlin, and the tiger shark. The record yellowfin weighed 318 pounds, the bluefin 758 pounds, and the tiger shark and blue marlin over 1,000 pounds each. Having fished for nothing larger than Chinook salmon, I did not fully realize the magnitude of his accomplishment until I saw a portfolio of photographs of him with these monsters.

Reading his accounts of the harrowing, bone-wrenching struggles with these fish, some of which were epic battles of more than five hours, is like being at his side in the boat. I smelled the flying-fish bait on the salt air and the whirling reel smoking when a big one sounded for the bottom. I heard the sharp crack as another rod broke and felt Grey's agony when a fish snapped the line after hours of battle.

If he had been a fisherman only, it is doubtful that many would still remember the name Zane Grey. The fame of a fisherman is usually ephemeral, living on in the oral accounts of friends or family, fading to silence with the indifference of succeeding generations that have their own fish stories to tell. A few fishermen, like Grey, make the record books, only to have their names supplanted with the passage of time.

Lasting fame is harder to come by. Zane Grey's name lives on because a river of words flowed from his pen. In the span of his career, he wrote 61

Zane Grey with world-record bluefin tuna*

novels. The articles he produced for various magazines were legion. *Field and Stream* alone published 28 articles and five long serials. He published nine nonfiction books about his fishing adventures, which in my opinion contain much of his best writing.

While on his fishing expeditions, Grey journalized extensively on a daily basis, which made it possible for him to later recapture the subtle nuances of scenery or the exact tackle he was using when he caught a particular fish. This practice resulted in accounts that are exciting, personal, and descriptive in a highly visual, colorful, even painterly way. For a man considered vain and overly serious by some who met him, Grey wrote fishing tales that are surprisingly full of humor and self-mockery. In *Tales of Fresh Water Fishing,* he wrote, "These Rogue River steelhead must have had a council before my arrival to decide upon the infinitely various and endless tricks they would play upon me. To be sure, they played a few upon my comrades, but the great majority, and the hopeless ones and terrible ones, fell to my lot."

Grey landed his first steelhead at Chair Riffle on the Rogue in 1922. "Then my rod sprang down, straightened by a violent tug, so energetic and electrifying that I was astounded. The scream of my reel told me what had happened." This was a seminal moment in Grey's career as a fisherman and, to a lesser extent, as a writer. He continued to pursue steelhead in southern Oregon for the rest of his life, first on the Rogue and later on the Umpqua.

Zane Grey wrote voluminously about the Rogue and its fishing. In *Tales of Fresh Water Fishing,* he devotes 169 pages — nearly two-thirds of the book—to steelhead fishing on the Rogue, far more than to any other freshwater stream, including the beloved Lackawaxen Creek of his boyhood. Of catching that first steelhead at Chair Riffle, he continues:

Above Chair Riffle

If moments could be wholly all-satisfying with thrills and starts, and dreads and hopes, and vague, deep, full sense of the wild beauty of the environment, and the vain boyish joy in showing my comrades my luck and skill—if moments of life could utterly satisfy, I experienced them then. It took what seemed a very long time to tire and lead that steelhead, but at last I accomplished it....That was the moment to have released him. I had the motive, but not the unselfish appreciation of him and his beautiful Rogue, not that time. He had been too hard to catch and there across the river stood those comrades of mine. Instead I lifted him up in the sunlight for them to see.

This confessional passage is utterly revealing of the writer's times and his deepest motives. On display are his pride, his love of nature, his developing consciousness toward the environment and the conflict he felt. Like Saint Augustine who prayed, "God make me holy, but not yet," Grey could not release that first steelhead.

While Grey's love of fishing and nature was instinctual, his predilections as a conservationist developed more slowly. Conservationism, an orientation so out of step with the industrial juggernaut exploiting the natural resources of America in his day, and ours for that matter, was just beginning to dawn in the hearts and minds of a few outstanding men. Fortunately for Grey, he was able to come into contact with some of the most important of these men through his participation in an outdoors organization in New York called the Camp Fire Club.

Among the members of the club were the author William T. Hornaday, who promoted game preserves and became director of the New York Zoological Park, and the artist and writer Ernest Thompson Seton, cofounder of the Boy Scouts of America. Gifford Pinchot, Yale professor of forestry, also belonged. He was a friend of the founder of the Sierra Club, John Muir, and confidant and advisor to Theodore Roosevelt, also a Camp Fire Club member.

It was Pinchot who coined the word "conservation," which Roosevelt adopted and made the centerpiece of his administration. With Pinchot at his side, Roosevelt moved to convert 194 million acres of scenic public land into national parks, including the Grand Canyon, Niagara Falls, Mesa Verde, and Crater Lake, the headwaters of the Rogue River.

Zane Grey coined his own phrase in appealing for conservation. He used the title *Vanishing America* for an article that appeared in the news organ of the Isaac Walton League, a conservation organization which he co-founded in 1922. The phrase appears again in *Tales of Freshwater Fishing*. In a conversation Grey had with a resident gold miner along the Rogue at Whiskey Creek, both men decry the Forest Service's plan to cut military and fire roads down the Rogue. "But all wilderness dwellers, hunters and fishermen, and lovers of the forest, hate automobile roads, and know they are one great cause, probably the greatest, of our vanishing America."

Grey occasionally introduced conservationist themes indirectly in his Western novels by casting the story line against the backdrop of an environmental issue. A good example is *Rogue River Feud*, the story of a young man returned from war who reclaims his life on the river and falls in love in the process. The novel is an interplay between the love story and the protagonist's struggles as an independent commercial fisherman. The historical context was the early twentieth-century conflict between the upriver fishermen on the Rogue and Robert Hume's canning monopoly at the mouth of the river, which was threatening their livelihood and the future of the salmon runs.

Rogue River Feud is not considered one of Grey's strongest novels. Grey scholar Joe Wheeler, of the Center for the New West, has written, "It is really Grey's own personal love letter to one of his favorite rivers." As such, in addition to historical accuracy, it contains wonderful descriptions of the river. Its authenticity is largely the result of all the time Grey spent on the Rogue.

Today, Grey's legacy as a conservationist is becoming more apparent. Todd Newport, the current president of the Zane Grey's West Society, has written, "We need to continue to protect historical sites and important wilderness for generations to come. This is something with which I feel Zane Grey would have very much agreed. He certainly was an environmentalist ahead of his time." Thanks indirectly to Grey's writing, which canonized the river for its beauty and sport fishing, the Rogue was ultimately included among the first eight rivers in America to have large sections protected under the Wild and Scenic Rivers Act.

If you are lucky enough to make a trip down the Rogue and wish to do a further meditation on the man whose writing is largely responsible for the river's reputation outside of Oregon, you will want to stop at Winkle Bar. Zane Grey's cabin is still intact, thanks to the Levi-Strauss family, which purchased the property and preserved it. They have given the public access to the site, in part with the hope that it might be an inspiration to young writers. They did the same with Hemingway's cabin in Idaho.

Located in the heart of the Wild and Scenic section of the river, the cabin at Winkle Bar can be reached only by boat or on foot from the Rogue River Trail. Fishermen stop there to wet a line, rest, cool off, eat lunch, or simply to reminisce about Grey and his era. You can stretch out near the cabin at midday on the lush, green grass of this irrigated oasis, shaded from the intense summer sun by the venerable old oaks.

In my experience, the river at Winkle Bar can have a hypnotic effect, particularly if the fish are not biting. Maybe it's the remoteness of the place, where cell phones do not work, or maybe it's several days of exposure to the elements in getting there, the absorption in nature, or just the inexorable sweep of the river. The longer I stare at it, the more the river seems to flow in both directions, forward toward aspiration, my projects, the next fish, and backwards to the time of Zane Grey and my father. There's something in the air, too, a peacefulness that moved Grey to write:

And then, up and down Winkle Bar, I fished all of one of the briefest and happiest days I ever had. I cast and rested and watched the river and the mountains, and listened to the murmur of running water. Then I cast again. Where the hours sped I never knew. Not a sign of a strike or sign of a fish did I have! But that did not matter. There was something in the lonely solitude of the great hills, something in the comradeship of the river that sufficed for me.

Winkle Bar

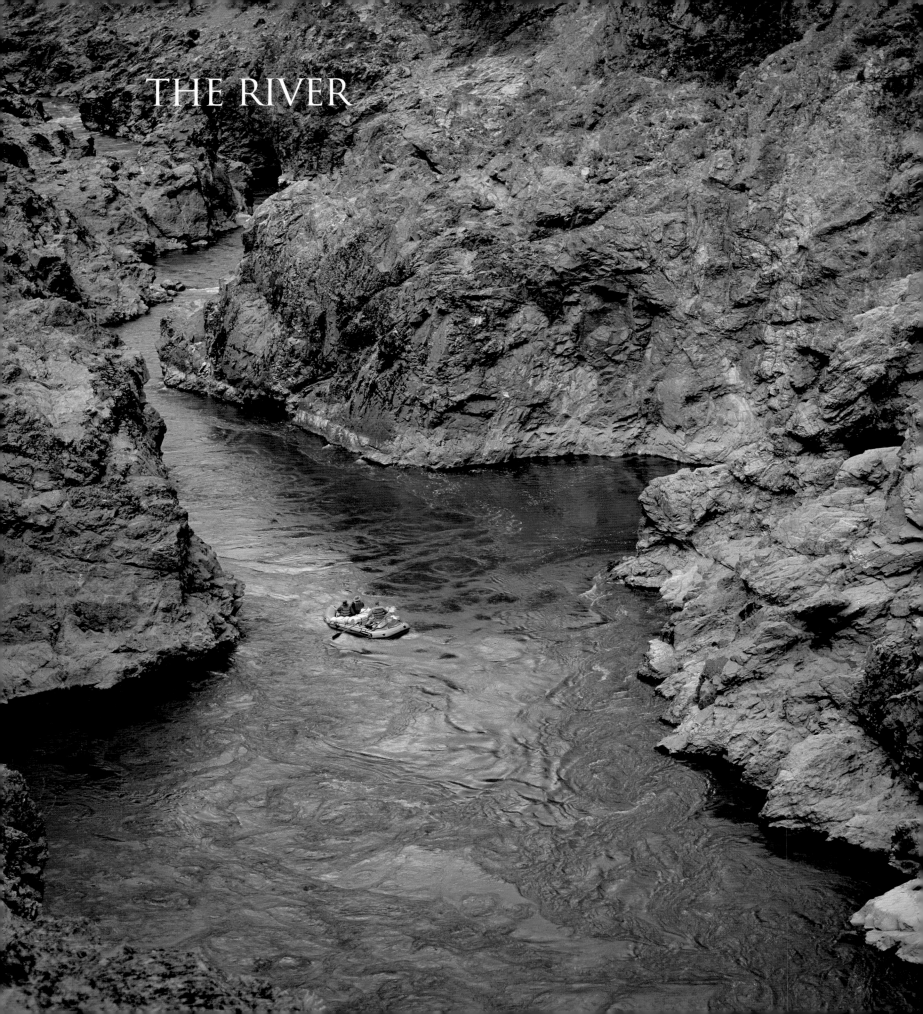

THE RIVER

FAR LEFT: *Mule Creek Canyon*
ABOVE: *Below Prospect*

THE RIVER AND TIME
A Brief Geologic History of the Rogue

To search for the geologic origins of the Rogue River is to look back over an ocean of time so vast that the rigors of science are reduced to speculation. Over 100 million years ago, long before the river was the river, there was a sea. There were no Homo sapiens then, but for the sake of this narrative imagine you are on that sea, one of a few shadowy figures in a cedar canoe, rising and falling with the pulse of time. Where the Rogue emerges from a mountainside in our present day, nothing but the dark water can be seen in any direction. Suddenly, as the canoe crests another mighty wave, someone spies a hint of land, like a mirage on the western horizon. An island!

Still visible today as a peak in the Klamath Mountains, this island had a long history before being sighted from the canoe. Approximately 250 million years ago, a vast section of the Pacific sea floor, part of the moving mosaic of the earth's crust called a tectonic plate, suddenly began drifting eastward on a collision course with the North American continent. At impact, the sea floor began pushing under the lighter continent. Islands in the Pacific were carried eastward with the moving sea floor and scraped off on the edge of the continent in succession during the next 100 million years. At least seven islands accumulated, forming an accreted mass that would eventually become a part of the Klamaths.

Until recently, there was no substantial theory for the triggering of the sea floor's sudden movement eastward. Then in 2001, scientists reported that in exposed sediments of the Triassic period in China, Japan, and Hungary, they had found unusual argon and helium gas molecules that could only be formed outside the earth's atmosphere. Evidence suggests that these molecules were delivered to earth by a huge asteroid, four to eight miles across, that struck the planet 250 million years ago. In all likelihood, this blow set in motion the section of the Pacific sea floor that collided with the North American continent. Perhaps it was not a coincidence that three continents, North America, Europe and Africa, separated and began to drift apart at approximately that same time.

From the perspective of your canoe, the exact timing and cause of the drifting of the Pacific sea floor and its collision with the continent matters little. What does matter is that the collision has set in motion cataclysmic geological events that will part the waters of the inland sea, giving rise to the dry land on which the Rogue had its genesis.

For perhaps 50 million years, the islands that became a part of the Klamaths were the southwestern portion of a chain of mountains, including the Blues and the Wallowas, that formed an early coastal range, several hundred miles to the east of the present-day Coast Range. As the early coastal mountains were forming, the eastward-moving sea floor sank farther beneath the continental plate, gradually melting as it pushed ever deeper toward the heat of the earth's core. Over the millennia, a subterranean sea of magma formed, which began resurfacing as a chain of volcanoes about 100 miles inland from the coastal mountains. Geologists know this pattern of nascent coastal mountains accompanied by inland volcanoes to be typical of a massive tectonic disturbance.

The early coastal range grew as volcanic material was added from the east and accumulating sediments were being scraped off on the western flank of the range by the movement of the sea floor. These conditions persisted in a relatively uninterrupted fashion until an estimated 125 million years ago, when the seven accreted Pacific islands that became part of the Klamaths grew wayward again. In a shape-shifting maneuver, the cause of which is unknown, they broke off from their sister mountains and drifted westward, becoming the offshore islands you have spied from your canoe.

The next major change was the onset of three volcanic events that laid the basis for Oregon's geography as we recognize it today. Thirty-five million years ago, the line of the sea floor's penetration beneath the continent abruptly shifted over 100 miles westward to near the line's present position off of our coast. Again, after an event of this magnitude, a new series of volcanoes soon appeared. These volcanic eruptions, the most violent the western continent has ever known, continued for nearly 20 million years, forming the early western Cascades. As these mountains were forming, the lighter material from the surface of the sea floor was pushing into the sea plains of the continental shelf along the new line of their interface, creating the present-day Coast Range. This mountain range was to the north and roughly in line with the Klamaths, which were also being uplifted and increased by the same geologic activity. Gradually, they linked up, forming the continuous stretch of mountains the length of Oregon that inland valley dwellers must drive through now to get to the beach.

Fast-forwarding to the present, you trade in your cedar canoe for a flashy red fiberglass white-water kayak. Deep in the heart of the Wild and Scenic section, you drift on the green waters of the Rogue, temporarily escaping the intense summer sun in the cool shadows of Mule Creek Canyon. While you are ashore at Stair Creek to explore its beautiful twin falls, you look across the river at the 200-foot-high cliffs of Inspiration Point and pose a question: How did the river find its way through these mountains? The answer is relatively simple.

The earliest volcanic eruptions that formed the western Cascades created the networks of runoff that support the existence of rivers. The early incarnations of two rivers in southwestern Oregon, the Rogue and its northerly sister, the Umpqua, began flowing westward prior to the uplift of the Klamath Mountains and the Coast Range. As these mountains uplifted, the preexisting rivers cut down through them, creating the narrow channels and steep river canyons, like Mule Creek, that we marvel at today.

The volcanic activity that formed the western Cascades is far from the end of the story in the creation of the present-day Rogue River. The next episode began about 20 million years ago, when floods of molten basalt began oozing up out of the earth in what is now north-central and north-eastern Oregon. This event, while not as dramatic as the earlier eruptions, was equally formative, creating a volcanic plateau of virtually the entire state, with the exception of the Cascades. Most likely, what remained of the old inland sea east of the Klamaths was filled in at this time, and with it the earliest incarnation of the Rogue. Over time, the Rogue reasserted itself, forming deep canyons to the west of its headwaters in the Cascades.

The most tangible evidence of the Rogue's shape and course during this period is found in an example of what geologists refer to as inverted topography. Stated simply, inverted topography occurs when features in the landscape that were formerly the lowest in elevation are raised up and become the highest. About seven million years ago, a lava flow originating near the headwaters scoured out the Rogue and filled in its canyons further down in the valley, forming hard igneous rock as it cooled. The Rogue was forced into a new course, leaving a virtual stone casting where it had flowed before in the canyons. As time went on, the softer material surrounding the casting was eroded away, leaving a meandering, inverted "river of stone" in the landscape. Its last remnants, the Table Rocks, are visible in the valley north of Medford.

The eruptions that filled the canyons in the Rogue Valley were part of the third volcanic phase in the forming of the Oregon landscape, which began 12 million years ago and had its most recent expression in the eruption of

Mount St. Helens in 1980. The past million years have been particularly active, producing the high volcanoes of the Cascades, such as Mount McLoughlin, Mount Hood, Mount Jefferson, and Mount Mazama, the point of origin of the Rogue River.

During the half million years of Mount Mazama's existence, the mountain and the river have had a restless relationship due to the mountain's many eruptions, each forcing the river, in varying degrees, to follow a new course. Mazama's most recent eruption, 7,700 years ago, laid the foundation for the upper Rogue's current reincarnation, the beautiful stream that bursts from the side of the mountain, tumbles off ledges to form numerous waterfalls, flows underground through lava tubes, and meanders through deep beds of volcanic ash. Here at its headwaters, the Rogue is a geologically young river on its way down to the valley and on to its ancestral channel through the Klamath Mountains. Like all rivers, the Rogue is always simultaneously beginning and ending, but unlike others, the path that it follows may be new or old, depending on where you put in your canoe.

Table Rock

THE FIRST PEOPLE ON THE ROGUE
The History of the Native Americans Living on the Rogue

Then I was standing on the highest mountain of them all, and round about beneath me was the whole hoop of the world. And while I stood there I saw more than I can tell and understood more than I saw; for I was seeing in a sacred manner the shapes of all things in the spirit, and the shape of all shapes as they must live together like one being. And I saw that the sacred hoop of my people was one of many hoops that made one circle, wide as daylight and as starlight, and in the center grew one mighty flowering tree to shelter all the children of one mother and one father. And I saw that it was holy.

—BLACK ELK, OGLALA SIOUX
Black Elk Speaks

The powerful light of wisdom, compassion, understanding, and tolerance still emanates from the shamanic vision of Black Elk long after his people and the bison that sustained them were driven to near extinction by the white men during the late 1800s. The Native Americans who inhabited the Rogue River country a few decades earlier suffered a similar, if not worse, fate. The Oglala were at least placed on a reservation in the Black Hills, their homeland, while the bands from the Rogue were forced onto reservations over 200 miles to the north of their traditional lands. Uprooted from their culture, an exhausted people, many blind, lame, and ill, endured a difficult journey, mostly on foot, to an unfamiliar region where they were thrown together with the survivors of other Oregon tribes that had very different cultures and languages.

Of the approximately 10,000 Native Americans living along and in the vicinity of the Rogue at the beginning of the nineteenth century, fewer than 2,000 survived the encounter with the white culture that culminated in the war of 1855-56. The white man's decimation of the Plains Indians, and the buffalo that provided the Indians' main food source, had a parallel in the Rogue country. Within less than 100 years after the defeat of the Rogue Indians, the salmon runs that had sustained the people on the Rogue for millennia were all but gone.

Why emphasize the plight of the Native Americans who lived along the Rogue in a book purporting to be a celebration of the river? The fundamental reasons for telling their story begin with longevity. They have been here far longer than the present culture. Carbon-dated shards found at Battle Bar on the lower Rogue prove that people have lived along the river's shores for at least 9,000 years. But they were not just one tribe, not just Rogues, as the singular name given to them by the French fur trappers suggests.

There were many hoops in the circle of Native people living along the Rogue. Because of the rugged terrain they inhabited and the subsistence level of their lives, Native people tended to live in small bands or family groups of 30 to 150 people, rather than the larger political entities we think of as tribes. Their diversity is perhaps most easily spoken about in terms of their languages.

At the mouth of the Rogue was the largest group, the Tututini, meaning "people close to the river" in the Athapascan dialect they spoke. The bands along Galice Creek and along the Applegate and Shasta Costa tributaries also spoke Athapascan dialects. The core language of these people was spoken by Natives as far north as the Yukon and as far south as Arizona and New Mexico. There were Athapascan speakers at the mouth of the Columbia, in the Umpqua watershed just north of the Rogue, and along the Smith and Klamath Rivers to the immediate south.

Inland, in the valley between the Coast Range and the Cascades, was the second-largest language group, the Takelman. Their language was totally unique, bearing no resemblance to the languages of the tribes surrounding their homeland or anywhere in western Oregon, a phenomenon ethnologists have been unable to explain. The Takelman speakers were divided into two dialect groups: the Dagelmas ("those living along the river") and the Latgawas ("those living in the uplands"). A third major language group, the Shastan, was spoken by Natives whose home territory was south along the Klamath River of northern California. Some of these people had crossed the Siskiyous and taken up residence in the Rogue watershed along Jenny Creek and Bear Creek in what is now Jackson County.

By the mid-1830s, all of the diverse bands of Native Americans living on the river were called Rogues by the whites coming into the area. By labeling the Native people in that fashion, the white men effectively, if unwittingly, stripped them of their identities. Replacing the traditional Native names with a reductive stereotype prejudiced whites coming into the area and eventually served the purpose of extermination.

The word "extermination" was used frequently at the time by whites describing the only alternative when dealing with the local Indians. It became the banner of some of the Oregon Volunteers who came together to get rid of the Indians of the Rogue country. This group, composed primarily of gold miners, repeatedly provoked warfare with the Indians by its attacks on villages, abuse of Indian women, and callous disregard for the presence of the U.S. Army and the Bureau of Indian Affairs. There were also citizens in southern Oregon who were more fair-minded and extended the hand of friendship to the Native Americans. These well-meaning whites were a distinct minority, and their protests against the extremists were unorganized and ineffectual.

Another reason for examining the history of the Native Americans on the Rogue is the imbalance in the historical record depicting their character and point of view, particularly in regard to their relations with the whites. Because the bands along the Rogue preserved their culture orally, they left no written record. Consequently, we have only half of the story, which has to be pieced together from U.S. Army correspondence, Bureau of Indian Affairs papers, diaries, letters, and early newspapers. This original research was most thoroughly done by Stephen Dow Beckham, who concluded that for "too long had the racist narratives pointed to the Rogue Indians as 'savages' and 'barbarians'."

Of course, the Rogues were not saints. Although they were considered primarily peaceful by the surrounding tribes in the region, they occasionally fought with other Indians who came into their territory. Descriptions of battles between the Rogues and Shastas, however, suggest a type of warfare different than that practiced concurrently in Europe, or in our country's Civil War, where masses of troops charged headlong at one another, often resulting in great loss of life.

The tribal wars among the Indians of the Pacific Northwest were characterized by displays of strength, skill, and bravery, rather than the mere counting of dead bodies at day's end. If a warrior made a spirited attack on the enemy camp, striking several wounding blows and then escaping, the passion of his outrageous act might signal to the enemy that even though they possessed superior numbers, their quarrel with the warrior's band could be disastrous. At that point, negotiations might be started or the whole contention simply written off. In *Requiem for a People*, Beckman describes a "mock-heroic" battle between Shastas from the Klamath River and Shastas living along Bear Creek that had a theatrical quality, allowing for the establishment of a clear victor with woundings, but no loss of life.

It seems that in warfare, as in their daily life of hunting and gathering, the Native people practiced an economy of means. It is not too far-fetched to suggest that they did not wish to waste the lives of their people or the lives of other indigenous people who, in their world view, were of the same mother, the Earth. However, their shared-earth philosophy did not preclude stealing from other tribes, which was looked upon more as a sport, although at times it resulted in confrontation.

Warfare with those who did not share their code of battle was a different story. The Indians did not turn the other cheek to the whites, who shot to kill. They matched brutality for brutality, murder for murder, in their retribution and revenge against the aliens who seemingly had come to destroy their traditional way of life. During the wars with the whites, the Rogues proved to be fearless warriors, particularly the people living inland, who, in the estimation of the U.S. Army, had tactical sophistication not generally found among other tribes in the region. This added to the reputation they had earned earlier as a people particularly fierce when wronged. Many of their savage attacks against the settlers in the Rogue Valley are detailed in *Until the Last Arrow*, Percy T. Booth's exhaustive account of the Rogue River Indian wars.

What Black Elk called "the darkness in (white) men's eyes" sealed the fate of most of the western tribes in America. Apologists have written off this sad episode in our nation's history as the unfortunate collision between a Stone Age people and the juggernaut of the white world's sense of manifest destiny. Now this view is changing. In a courageous statement made in 2001, Kevin Grover, head of the Bureau of Indian Affairs, rendered an apology

*Jennie**

for his agency's participation in the "ethnic cleansing" that befell the western tribes. He further stated that the atrocities perpetrated against the Native people made for a tragedy so ghastly that it cannot be dismissed as merely the inevitable clash between competing ways of life. This point of view is certainly borne out by the most accurate accounting of the conflicts between the Native people and the whites in the Rogue Valley.

Although they warred with the whites, the various bands along the river tended to get along well with each other, often sharing the same favored fishing spots. In their intermingling, it was not uncommon for a young woman from one band to marry a man from a band that spoke a different dialect or language. The unions, which promoted harmony in the region, were a cause for celebration and gift-giving between the two parties. Great feasts were also held to honor the headmen of tribes from other regions. These state dinners often brought together several bands that would act as host for the foreign guests. Through several days of feasting, the hosts would display their generosity and abundance. Under an umbrella of hospitality, they mixed pleasure, business, and politics, while sending the message that they were a strong people not to be underestimated.

The people of the Rogue could be playful as well. Among the favorite pastimes were the shinny games (similar to cricket), the tossing of gambling sticks, and storytelling. Along with stories about the mythological trickster, Coyote, there were tales about Tar-Baby and Loon-Woman. The stories explained the existence of prominent features in the landscape and accounted for natural phenomena. The storms that thrashed the coastline were said to be caused by the evil ocean-dwelling spirit, Seatco. Great philosophical issues were played out in dialogue between characters like Coyote and Roasting-Dead-People, a large, black, long-legged beetle that represented death.

Like most indigenous cultures, the culture of the Native Americans along the Rogue was one of memory and maintenance. They remembered perennially their connection to nature and maintained their way of life by performing rituals. Though little of their original culture remains, we know that all the bands on the Rogue had songs and ceremonies honoring the salmon. There was a ritual performed with the taking of the first salmon from the spring run in order to acknowledge the spirits and maintain the bounty they provided. Traditionally, the first salmon caught by a young man was not eaten by his immediate family, but offered to others in the band. Such practices emphasized the importance of the group over its individual members. For millennia, the Native people found joy, suffered, wondered, loved, hated, searched, played, fought, made peace, gave birth, and died in turn through an endless time recalled in the story of a people that went on and on like the green river that gave them life.

The earliest written records of contacts between the whites and the Native people living at the mouth of the Rogue indicate that the Native people were friendly. At Cape Blanco, in 1792, Tututini men paddled their narrow canoes carved from single cedar logs through the surf and into the open sea to visit ships from an exploratory expedition out of Vancouver. In a remarkable gesture, possibly intended to display their openness and harmless intent, the men took off their clothing, made primarily from deer skin and the hides and fur of other small game, and boarded the ships naked. Archibald Menzies, a botanist aboard the vessel, Chatham, wrote in his journal that the Tututini men were "nowise sullen or distrustful" in their behavior. Seeing past the Tututini's nakedness, tattoos, and pierced noses and ears, Menzies states clearly that the Tututini showed "mild and peaceable dispositions."

How different was Menzies' assessment of the Tututini from that of another white man aboard a different ship that was in the area during the same month and year. Captain Robert Gray's trading expedition to the southern Oregon coast encountered the Tututini off Cape Blanco, too, and bartered successfully with them. The trading for sea otter skins was said to be mutually agreeable, so there is no reason to imagine tensions between the two parties or a different demeanor on the part of the Tututini than that experienced by Menzies. However, John Boit, a shipmate of Gray's, wrote in his journal after meeting the Tututini, "I'm fearful these fellows are cannibals." Two men of the same culture had met an indigenous people: Boit with fearfulness, and Menzies with an open mind. A bit of the "darkness in men's eyes" is already present in Boit's xenophobic reaction, the beginnings of distrust and misunderstanding. The Tututini lived off of the salmon in the river, not off of human flesh.

We have no way of knowing what transpired between the Tututini and the fur traders in the ensuing years. The record is incomplete, but another journal entry suggests that trouble began to come to the peaceful people along the Rogue.

Twenty-five years after the voyage of the Chatham, the British vessel Columbia sailed into the same turbulent waters off Cape Blanco with the intent of trading for hides of the rapidly vanishing sea otter. In what had become routine, the Tututini paddled their narrow canoes out to the sailing ships through the dangerous waters. It is likely that some of the Tututini were the sons of men who had paddled out to the Chatham in curiosity a quarter century before.

With the eyes of Peter Corney, who witnessed their approach from the deck of the Columbia and recorded the event in his journal, we see the Indians raising bunches of green boughs and feathers. One of them, possibly the head man of their band, offers a speech which, of course, no one on board understands. The Tututini men begin singing loudly as their canoes near the side of the ship. The crew of the Columbia lowers ropes for the Indians to aid them aboard, but, according to Corney, the Tututini seem terrified at the prospect and refuse the welcome. Clearly, mutual fear and mistrust were beginning to shroud the relations between the Native people and the whites coming into the region.

As more explorers, entrepreneurs, miners, and farmers came into the Rogue country, the panic of the Natives over the threat to their way of life grew into open hostility toward the new arrivals. While the Tututini people at the mouth of the Rogue tried to maintain harmony with the whites, the Indians in the interior valleys began to fight practically every incursion into their territory. Their efforts to keep their lands free of the foreigners inspired the French trappers to call them the Rogues.

The Latgawas of the upper river displayed a passionate spirit of resistance that earned them the reputation as the fiercest band. This isolated group lived on a stretch of the Rogue where limited food sources made the balance of daily survival more precarious than for their counterparts on the coast, where fish, mussels, and eatable plants were more bountiful, and clams and crabs were also available. In the eyes of the Latgawas, the arrival of strange people in their valley, who would be competing for the food available, must have been seen as a matter of life or death. For years, their struggle kept the enemy at bay. Southwest Oregon was the last area of the state to be settled. But eventually the wealth to be gained there, along with the momentum of the westward expansion, brought whites in overwhelming numbers.

Although much of the trading for sea otter and beaver pelts along the coast was initially conducted in an amicable fashion, in the process the traditional ways of the Native Americans were destabilized dramatically. An innocent people who hoarded nothing stared into the insatiable belly of the beast. While the animal skins they used for warmth and ceremony were being shipped as adornments all over the world for profit they would never see, the Tututini were fascinated by tiny bronze bells from China, metal buttons, and thimbles offered them in trade.

Anything made from the mysterious, heavy substance that was harder than any rock captivated the people of a Stone Age culture and became their obsession. Metal could reflect sunlight, be sharpened, or made into many shapes, even serpent-sticks that spit fire and could kill. In 1850, while one of their band sawed with a bone knife on the anchor chain, Indians attempted to strip the copper plating from the hull of the vessel Samuel Roberts as she lay in the harbor at the mouth of the Rogue. In all likelihood, they believed that the power of the strangely dressed men who came from far away on their huge, magnificent ships was contained in the metal they possessed. It is not an exaggeration to say that in order to create a shock in our culture equivalent to what the Tututini were experiencing, we must imagine being introduced to an unknown element or technology by aliens from outer space.

It wasn't copper or iron though, but a different metal that was responsible for the wars that resulted in the slaughter and banishment of the Native American people along the Rogue. Black Elk called it "the yellow metal that made the white men crazy," and the white men's lust for it brought terrible violence against the Ogala Sioux, as it did against the Indians on the Rogue. The Indians had no use for the gold that shone in the sands of the river and its tributary streams. Their indifference to it was clearly demonstrated in 1850, when Latgawas raided the camp of miners returning from the gold fields of California. Among the articles they stole were several pouches of gold dust. It was later learned that they dumped the gold dust into the river, but retained the fine leather pouches that were their prize.

In January of 1852, two mule skinners, James Cluggage and John Pool, headed south through the winter rain with a team carrying supplies from Scottsburg, on the Umpqua, to miners in the gold fields of northern California. When they reached the Rogue Valley, they made camp near the Table Rocks. The mules were set out to graze in the meadows along the river, and two of them wandered off. In the wet terrain, Cluggage and Pool easily found the mules' tracks along a creek feeding the Rogue and followed their trail westward. As the narrowing creek climbed into the hills, gold dust glistened in the shallows, and there were nuggets for the picking laced along the stream. Cluggage and Pool changed professions on the spot and soon were consuming the supplies intended for the miners in California. During the first weeks and months of the strike, they were said to have averaged about 100 ounces of gold a day. The historical record is unclear as to whether the men found their mules.

Although it wasn't the first gold found in the Rogue Valley, it was the richest strike, and the news couldn't be contained. By spring, Cluggage and Pool were joined by hundreds of miners who came up from northern California. Coincidentally, Jackson County, named after the seventh president of the United States, Andrew Jackson, had been established during the same month the strike took place. The county encompassed the gold-bearing stream, which was dubbed Jackson Creek, and Jacksonville, the boom town created by the strike. The gold rush opened the floodgates to change.

The influx of miners brought laborers and suppliers as well. Placer mining—the panning and sluicing of gold from the river and creeks—gradually gave way to excavation, creating a need for beams and planks, which engendered the early logging industry. Settlers who wanted to ranch and farm in the Rogue Valley found strength in the number of miners there and began moving to the valley, as well. Their hogs rooted out the camas bulbs in the meadows along the Rogue, diminishing a major food source for the Native people.

The settlers near the coast, who wanted a ready source of timber for their split-rail fences and cabins, also prevented the Indians from burning hillsides along the river there. Burning had been done for centuries as a gesture we can only surmise was expressive of their values and as such was integral to their culture. From the practical standpoint, it aided in creating an open terrain for seed gathering and the hunting of game. The settlers fenced much of this open land and plowed under the grasses, eliminating the seed harvest that had helped sustain the Native people.

The worst environmental effect of the gold mining industry was the impact on the river itself and the salmon in particular, which was the primary food source for the Native people. Hundreds of miners turned over gravel bars with picks and shovels, digging in the tributary streams that were sometimes completely rerouted to feed sluice boxes or to make a vein of gold easier to reach. Dynamite was occasionally used to remove boulders and

*Mary **

eventually to create mine shafts. The turbulence in the water, combined with the destruction of gravel bars and tributary streams, interrupted the reproductive cycle of the salmon. The Rogue, which normally flowed crystal clear after the winter rain and melt-off, was perpetually muddied during the years that mining took place.

The miner's physical hunger also threatened the food supply of the Native people. The miners wanted meat to sustain them through the long hours of hard labor, and the deer and elk populations provided for their needs. Ralph Train, a fourth-generation descendant of the first settlers in the Shady Cove area, tells of his father, Orin, working a stint as hunter for the Lone Star mining operation on the upper river during the early 1900s. Orin's charge was to kill three deer a day, which he did dutifully for the year and a half he worked for the operation.

Gold miner (Josephine County) circa 1910*

By far, the most degrading and dangerous impact of the mining industry on the Native people was the character of the miners themselves. They tended to be footloose men from many parts of the world, who were intent on getting rich quickly in a region that was as lawless as it was open. The malady they suffered from was referred to as gold fever. It left them with little patience for anything standing between them and their rapacious pursuit of the precious metal. Evidence of their hard-drinking ways was left in the names they gave tributaries, such as Booze Creek, Whiskey Creek, and Rum Creek. America Rollins Butler, an early settler in the upper Rogue Valley, wrote in her diary of 1853 that the miners in the volunteer militia "get drunk, sware, fight and disgrace themselves as rational beings." That same year, Lieutenant George Crook, who later became famous as a frontier general, was called up with troops from Fort James in northern California to intervene in the hostilities taking place in southern Oregon between the Indians and the volunteers. Crook was obligated by his job description to take the side of the volunteers, but his heart was not completely in the cause. Later, he wrote that "it was of no infrequent occurrence for an Indian to be shot down in cold blood, or a squaw to be raped by some brute. Such a thing as a white man being punished for outraging an Indian was unheard of. It was the fable of the wolf and the lamb every time."

Of course, there were miners with more generous temperaments. Some of them had no use for the Indians, but did not side with those intent on extermination. It was a plea to the Indian agent in the Rogue Valley by some prospectors that brought the troops up from Fort James. But, like the well-intentioned citizens who wrung their hands in Jacksonville while a mob of miners lynched a seven-year-old Indian boy in August of 1853, the responsible minority could not hold sway in the face of the venom of the exterminators. Call it ethnic cleansing or call it extermination, what happened to the Native people of southern Oregon during the years between 1853 and their placement on the reservations outside their homeland in 1856 was genocide, plain and simple. What had become a very tenuous coexistence spiraled out of control as fears, attacks, retribution, and revenge on both sides brought on outright war.

Ironically, in the few years just prior to the war, there had been signs that peace was possible between the indigenous people and the whites. In 1850, territorial governor General Joseph Lane negotiated an agreement with the Latgawas. He promised to place a permanent agent in the Rogue Valley to maintain peace and aid in protecting the Indians from unwarranted attacks. In addition, there was to be a yearly distribution of gifts to the Latagwa if they desisted in attacking parties passing through the valley and returned stolen property. Other agreements followed, but the situation continued to deteriorate. By 1852, the leaders of the Native people, realizing the need for more formal protection, accepted the inevitability of sharing their homeland with the whites. Two brothers, Toquahear, called Chief Sam by the whites, and Apserkaher, referred to as Joe, and a third leader named Anachaharah, or Jim, negotiated with General Lane, who was then commander of the volunteers. The headmen agreed to a reservation along the Evans Creek watershed, which included Upper Table Rock and a section of the Rogue from there south to the mouth of Evans Creek. The vast majority of the Rogue Valley was ceded to the whites for $6,000, of which $1,500 was to be paid in damages to various settlers.

During this period, there were many individual examples of Native people attempting to integrate peacefully into the white community. Some took jobs as servants in Jacksonville, while others began to show an interest in planting and raising crops. Even after having been repeatedly attacked on their reservation, the Indians at times showed good will and a desire for peace. On at least one occasion during the war of 1853, the Takelmas brought water to the wounded white men they had been facing on the battlefield and assisted in transporting them 25 miles for treatment.

The winter of 1855 was the coldest anyone could remember in the Rogue Valley. Snow depths on the valley floor reached 18 inches and, at one point, a stretch of the Rogue at Vannoys Ferry froze solidly enough that men and their horses were able to cross. During this time, Joel Palmer, the Superintendent of Indian Affairs, pushed ahead with a plan to remove the bands of Native people in the Rogue Valley to the Grande Ronde Reservation in Yamhill County, along with Umpqua, Mollala, and Calapuya bands from the north. Many in the Territorial House of Representatives opposed the plan, siding instead with the miners who advocated extermination and the settlers who had been attacked by the Indians and wanted revenge. They hated Palmer, but he was determined to seize what he saw as a last chance for these bands. Not only were the bands ravaged by war and still under frequent attack, but their food sources had been drastically depleted and they were without resistance to the white man's diseases.

In the early months of 1856, the relocation of the people began. In the bitter cold of that winter, under military protection, 400 Native people from the Table Rock Reservation started the trek of over 200 miles to the north. Under those conditions, the journey out of the Rogue Valley and through the Umpqua Mountains by itself would be daunting even to the able bodied. For the malnourished and infirm Native American survivors of the war, it was another blow to those already down. Their descendants today call this event Oregon's Trail of Tears. But even at this devastating low point for a people, there was a faint glimmer of hope, an indication of their ultimate survival. On the journey to the new reservation, eight people died and eight more were born.

Not all of the members of the valley bands were subject to the long march to the reservation that winter. Many fled down the Rogue into the canyons of what is now the Wild and Scenic section of the river. These survivors continued to fight on for their homeland, finding some refuge with bands who were indigenous to that area. Their hope faded fast. By June of 1856, those who had not been slaughtered on their way downriver surrendered at Big Bend, along with members of the coastal bands. Under armed guard, they walked to Port Orford, where they boarded the ship Columbia that carried them on the first leg of their journey, ending with a forced march through the hills of the Coast Range to a second northern reservation at Siletz.

Another group of Native people to leave the area that summer was under the leadership of a headman referred to as Old John, who resisted until the bitter end. After it surrendered, this band of around 200 walked a distance of 240 miles up the coast to Siletz. Stragglers from the bands on the Rogue who were hidden in the forests up and down the river, as well as those who fled the reservation shortly after arrival, were hunted down and summarily killed.

In their defeat, the Tututini, along with the inland Native bands, had inflicted a severe blow to the white settlements on the coast. They burned most of Gold Beach to the ground at one point and for a short while held their native territory once again. But the combined forces of government troops brought into the area from northern California and Port Orford, along with the local volunteers, turned the tide against them. The leaders of the Native people saw the end coming and agreed to the surrender at Big Bend. Even in defeat and surrender, the Indians continued to be attacked by the volunteers, who might have realized their goal of extermination had it not been for the tireless efforts of Joel Palmer, who once again was in the thick of it, conferring with the headmen of the bands to negotiate the surrender. His efforts, along with the good faith of the headmen and the stabilizing presence of military officers who wished to avoid a slaughter of the Indians, averted an even worse disaster for the Native people.

A great change had come to the Rogue River country. With the defeat and removal of the Native people, an indigenous culture fully adapted to and compatible with the natural environment had been supplanted by a culture based on the values and traditions of Europe.

Before the coming of the white men, indigenous cultures developed naturally on the plains, in the forests, and in the river valleys. They existed throughout America for thousands of years, much in the way native plants are able to adapt to a specific environment and survive there. Along the Rogue, survival was possible for those who lived humbly, taking from the river only in proportion to their needs and giving back through their rituals and reverent attitude toward their mother, the Earth. In their world view, the Great Spirit, the People, the River, and the Salmon were sacred and formed a circle. To remove one link in the circle was to break it, threatening the balance and leaving its life-sustaining promise unfulfilled.

The cultures of Europe were based on a very different premise. Their relationship to nature was graphically expressed in the biblical expulsion of Adam and Eve from the Garden of Eden. The expulsion gave rise to a sense of humans as separate, or separated, from nature, which in turn needed to be controlled and exploited for human purposes. With this viewpoint, the industrious European immigrants set out to conquer a vast country with seemingly unlimited natural resources, creating the wealthy nation we have inherited. Unfortunately, a sense of proportion in the taking of natural resources was absent from their world view, resulting in the degradation and threats to the environment we are faced with today.

*Rogue River Indians at Siletz Reservation**

Miners (Josephine County) circa 1910*

In light of the differences between the cosmology of the Native Americans and that of the new dominant culture, it is no wonder that the demise of the great salmon runs on the Rogue followed soon after the banishment of the Native people there. The sacred circle had been broken. Our scientific view of catastrophic events such as the near disappearance of a species invites debate and complicated explanations. From a spiritual standpoint, these explanations are tantamount to the disruption of a sacred interconnection.

The gold mining on the Rogue severely depleted the salmon runs during the years that it muddied the waters of the Rogue and disrupted and destroyed spawning habitat. Because this period was relatively short, the salmon recovered within a few years after the cessation of most of the mining activity. Unfortunately, the next resource to be exploited along the Rogue, with the onset of commercial fishing, was the salmon itself. Since then, the effects of damming the river, pollution, and logging have inhibited the return of the salmon in the numbers that once existed. In my view, as long as we continue to see salmon simply as a resource to be harvested, without honoring the species with the reverence held by the Native Americans, there is little chance for its recovery.

In spite of all their troubles, the life of the Dagelma, the Latgawas, the Tututini, and all the bands of Native Americans from the Rogue country is far from ended. We are waiting for more voices to emerge that will tell us of their long and difficult journey. Already, I have heard their gentleness in the beautiful songs of folk singer Snowball Butler, a descendant of the people from the valley, and their strength in the prayers offered at an annual powwow by Gilbert Towner, an elder of the Tututini. On another occasion, Gilbert said to me, "Whenever I see the river, I feel that it's part of my life's blood, and I believe our people feel the same way."

There are many descendants affiliated with the Siletz Tribe who in 2006 will conduct, for the twelfth consecutive year, a 240-mile relay run to the Rogue from Siletz, which culminates in a powwow near Agness. The run is part of an ongoing reconnection with the area on the part of the descendants, some of whom are also relearning the Athapascan language. In another example of the growing pride in their history and traditions, two men from the Grande Ronde Reservation recently walked the Trail of Tears from Table Rock to Grande Ronde in winter to call attention to the tragic event of 1856. In these examples, we can see that their culture still relies on memories kept alive for generations since their banishment. As Robert Kenta, the cultural coordinator for the Confederated Tribes of the Siletz, succinctly stated in 2000, "The people know where they came from."

I believe that the descendants of the first people on the Rogue belong in any discussion affecting the river's future. In accordance with their traditional philosophy, the people living along the Rogue's shores are connected to and inseparable from the river. This is a bond that transcends our narrow perspective of time and place to include everyone who has lived, is living, and will live along the Rogue. Whether we acknowledge it or not, we who share the river and the land are bound to it and share a common fate.

China Bar

WHAT'S IN A NAME?
How the River Became the Rogue

Naming things, that quintessential propensity of our species, can be a contentious business, reflective of our inclination as individuals to see things differently and to disagree. This has been particularly true when it comes to naming the surface features of the land here in the West, where the cussed and the self-righteous have only intransigence in common as they quarrel.

One hundred years ago, much of the West was still up for grabs, as were the geographic names that define it. Neighboring ranchers meeting in a land office to settle a boundary dispute argued over the name of a butte separating their property. Two miners staking claims on the same creek called it by different names. Unraveling the ensuing confusion is a painstaking business, as evidenced by volumes such as Lewis A. McArthur's *Oregon Geographic Names,* now in its sixth edition. This weighty tome of nearly 1,000 pages lists six historical periods of geographic naming, beginning with the period of "aboriginal Indian life" and ending with the "modern." The book documents many colorful accounts on the way to arriving at the names that are used today. It also clearly reveals that once the dissension over what to call a place ended, the argument over how the name arose in the first place began.

For the most part, the struggle over ownership and what to call features in the landscape has been laid to rest through property laws, the efforts of the U.S. Geological Survey, and extensive mapmaking. Still, a conundrum continues over the name of geologic features as predominant as a mountain range.

The case in point is the Klamath Range, which the Rogue River flows through on its way to the Pacific. People living in the Rogue Valley don't call the range the Klamaths; it is referred to as the Coast Range or the Siskiyous. Zane Grey referred to it as the Coast Range in his novel about the Rogue. All three names are correct, depending on your frame of reference. Geologists have always called the section of the Coast Range between the fortieth and forty-third parallels of latitude the Klamath Mountains, but geographers and mapmakers sometimes don't, and I have never heard the name in common usage.

A good example of the slipperiness and impermanence of naming in southern Oregon is Crater Lake, which was originally called, rather unimaginatively, Deep Blue Lake, and has also been known as Mysterious Lake, Lake Mystery, and Lake Majesty. Subject to the same kind of serial nomenclature is the singular volcanic peak on the eastern horizon of the Rogue Valley. For centuries, it was descriptively known to the Klamath Tribe as Mlaiksini Yaina, the mountain with steep sides. Then the early white settlers, in their plainspoken manner, began calling the mountain Snowy Butte or Big Butte. As the white culture attained dominance in the nineteenth century, the mountain was given two new names. On some regional maps of the mid-century, it appears as Mount Pit, a reference to the pits dug there by the Indians to trap game.

Shady Cove

During the same period, Hall J. Kelley, an early Oregon enthusiast and promoter, wanted to change the name of the Cascades to the President Mountains and give the southern Oregon peak the name Mount Adams. His idea seems to have gained some sway, resulting in the naming of northern peaks Mount Washington, Mount Jefferson, and Mount Adams. The Cascades, however, remained the Cascades, and in 1905, the peak in southern Oregon was officially designated Mount McLoughlin, after Dr. John McLoughlin, a prominent figure in the Hudson Bay Company who became powerful in the affairs of Oregon. Apparently, the mountain was not considered of presidential stature. Even after the official naming of Mount McLoughlin, there was slippage. I can remember many locals still referring to the mountain as Mount Pit during the years I was growing up.

Obviously, there is a dynamic interplay between the official and the vernacular when it comes to naming. While some wish to name big mountains after little men, others want to name them for the way they look. From the standpoint of common usage, practically every name of a site worth naming on the Rogue is in flux. Traditionally, the names have been ascribed by fishermen and river guides. Sometimes, part of the name remains, while a descriptive word changes to reflect some recent event. For example, Dugan's Hole became Telephone Hole (after Dugan got a phone?) and is currently called Mary's Pot Hole, or Surprise.

One thing is clear. From the mountain ranges—Klamath, Siskiyou, Cascade, and Umpqua—through the towns—Shady Cove, Gold Hill, Eagle Point, and Grants Pass—down to the creeks—Big Windy, Jump off Joe, Link Silver, and Flora Dell—the Rogue River country is rich in the poetry of names. You can hear the river's roar in the name Rough Rider Falls and hear its song where it turns at a place called Solitude. The names of the rapids, too—Rattlesnake, Wildcat, Devils Stairs, and Savage Rapids—fire the imagination and make the heart beat faster. Central in this litany is the name of the river itself.

The earliest written records we have regarding the name of the river come from two personal journals. The first was that of John Work of the Hudson Bay Company, recorded on September 16, 1833. In his entry of that date, he refers to the Rogue as River Coquin. This name did not originate with Work, but rather was taken from the French fur trappers who had been the first to regularly visit the interior of the Rogue country beginning in the late 1700s. The French word *coquin* translates into English as "rogue," "rascal," or "scoundrel." Because the early encounters between the trappers and the Native Americans living along the river were characterized by mistrust, misunderstanding, and trouble, the trappers began to refer to the river as the River of the Coquins.

In a later journal entry dated September 16, 1841, Henry Eld, of the Wilkes Expedition, refers to the river as the Rogue River and the Rascally River. Both names were obviously translations from the French. The name Rogue River became official in 1850 when William P. McArthur charted it as such for the U.S. Geological Survey.

In spite of these historical sources, the origin of the river's name has been disputed at various times. A popular misconception is that the name Rogue was derived from the French *rouge*, meaning *red*, even though the word does not appear anywhere in the early historical record. The explanation of this derivation is that in high water, when the river is churned up, it runs an earthy red color. The only problem is that it's not true, or, at best, is only partially true. Depending on which tributary creeks are flooding and the time of year, the river can appear to have a reddish cast. But in general, as any resident along the Rogue will attest, when the river floods, its color is just plain brown.

Since the time it became known as the Rogue, there has been only one serious attempt to rename the river. The gold rush on the Rogue inspired the Oregon Territorial Legislature of 1854 to rename it the Gold River. Their originality was met with defiance by the majority of citizens in southern Oregon, who seemed to have internalized some of the uncompromising spirit of the river. Exhibiting a strong sense of independence and local pride that exists in the region to this day, they ignored the edict and continued calling the river by its familiar name. In 1855, no doubt with a great deal of muttering and consternation, the legislature legally restored the name. The new handle would not fit, so the Rogue became the Rogue again.

SALMON AND THE ROGUE'S RECOVERY
Ecological Concerns and the History of the
Salmon Industry on the Rogue

For millennia, salmon sustained the lives of Native people living along the streams and great rivers of the Pacific Northwest. The Native cultures maintained the vital connection to the fish through ceremonies honoring the salmon and rituals supplicating their seasonal return. The interconnection linking the salmon, the people, the rivers, and the Great Mystery was considered sacred.

Today, our modern culture barely acknowledges the Native American descendants of the region or their sacred interconnection with the salmon. Neither do we fully acknowledge the salmon's importance in our own lives. We have allowed the coastal coho salmon to slip from the list of endangered species, even though their numbers are a fraction of what they were a century ago and their future is far from secure. Without ceremonies or rituals honoring the salmon, we tend to take their survival for granted, and few among us stop to consider a day when regional salmon may no longer be available in supermarkets or restaurants. We do not consider the species central to our survival, but when guests arrive from outside the Northwest, we serve them salmon, the quintessential fare defining our region.

It is not just good eating that links us with the salmon. Although we do not share the mythology of the Haida, the Native American carvers of the great totem poles, the salmon functions more than any other species as the totem animal of the Pacific Northwest. We may not believe that its blood is our blood, but its presence in our rivers and its reproductive journey inform our lives. In its cycle of birth, death, and rebirth, the salmon speaks to us of the deep rhythms of life, of continuity and renewal, interconnectedness, and our relationship with nature. Its struggle against the river's current is our own struggle against apathy and against the forces in the culture that champion profit over the health of our rivers and land and even over that of our own bodies. The salmon's self-sacrifice to procreate and sustain its offspring is a calling for us to consider future generations when seeking solutions to our cultural and environmental dilemmas.

Today, the Rogue River retains its wild, restless nature and much of its natural beauty. However, in spite of federal protection, a successful hatchery program, and our growing commitment to the environment, the Rogue, like many of the nation's rivers, remains endangered and in decline. Consider that there were once enough otter, mink, and beaver along the river to constitute an industry. Now the sea otters that formerly inhabited the mouth of the Rogue are extinct. River otters, mink, and beaver are protected by law, and a sighting of one of these rare animals can be the highlight of a journey down the river. Salmon runs in the past few years have rivaled any seen since the early 1950s, but compared to runs before that time, the salmon too are greatly depleted.

The salmon migrations of the early part of the twentieth century are legendary in the stories of the old-timers still living along the lower Rogue. Their parents spoke of runs so large they could be heard coming upstream. The sound, which Zane Grey termed a "souse" in his writings, was usually heard at night, when great schools of fish were on the move.

Some of the stories may be apocryphal, but there is much in the historical record to substantiate the old-timers' claims. On June 13, 1913, five driftboats out of Grants Pass using gill nets bagged 5,000 pounds of salmon in one day. At the end of the season, the Grants Pass *Daily Courier* reported that local gillnetters fishing the 15 miles of river between Grants Pass and Hog Creek had bagged over 100 tons of salmon. During that season, most fish were still being caught at the mouth of the river by cannery fishermen. Even if gillnetting was still permitted, such catches would be impossible today.

It is even more difficult to imagine the magnitude of the salmon runs before the degradation caused by gold mining in the 1850s. During the few years that the big rush was on in the Rogue country, entire creeks that provided spawning beds for thousands of fish were rerouted to provide water flow for the sluice boxes essential to placer mining. The mining activity also choked the river with silt that depressed the reproductive cycle of the fish. No sooner had the years of large-scale mining ended on the river and the salmon begun to recover than the 40-year history of heavy commercial fishing began on the Rogue.

The birth of the salmon-fishing industry on the Rogue resulted from the booming populations of San Francisco and Portland developing a taste for

Rogue gillnetters circa 1915*

salmon. At the same time, a huge demand for canned salmon was emerging in England. The market for salmon was so large by the late 1880s that Robert Hume of Astoria was able to establish a fishing enterprise of such magnitude at the mouth of the Rogue that he became known as the Salmon King of Oregon. Hume's land holdings gave his gillnetting fleet access to both sides of the river for 12 miles upstream from the ocean. Virtually controlling the entire fish population on the Rogue, Hume's company caught, processed, and shipped salmon from the river by the hundreds of tons over his 32-year career there. During its best five-year span from 1888 to 1892, the company hauled over five million pounds of salmon from the mouth of the Rogue.

Although Hume had shown no inclination toward preservation of the salmon during his earlier years of rapacious fishing on the Sacramento and Columbia Rivers, when he established his monopoly on the Rogue he showed a different side. Claiming motives higher than a selfish desire to ensure the survival of his empire in perpetuity, Hume began experimenting with artificial propagation of salmon not long after he arrived on the Rogue. In 1877, he built his first crude hatchery at Ellensburg, now known as Gold Beach.

Hume had mixed success over the years of salmon propagation at the mouth of the river. The claim has been made that eggs from the salmon caught at the coast were not mature enough for propagation. This notion is borne out by Hume's success after he began shipping eggs to his coastal hatchery from the upper river Rogue-Elk hatchery, which he helped develop along with the United States Fish Commission in 1897. This was a significant achievement for those days and certainly speaks volumes about Hume's will and grandiosity of vision.

Initially, the surplus eggs from the new hatchery 150 miles upriver were packed in 25-pound crates of wet moss. The crates were placed in larger boxes which were then filled with ice and sawdust to prevent the hatching process from beginning en route. From the hatchery, the egg-filled boxes were hauled by horse-drawn wagon to Medford, where they were entrained aboard the Southern Pacific bound for either Portland or San Francisco. After arrival in port, the cargo was placed aboard steamer ships. The eggs were then shipped to the Hume facility at the mouth of the Rogue, where they were hatched.

Although Hume's efforts to replenish the salmon population on the Rogue no doubt were to the benefit of all the fishermen on the river, he was still hated by the upriver fishermen. In their eyes, he was taking far more than his share of fish at the mouth of the Rogue. They also accused him of robbing eggs from the Rogue-Elk Hatchery, which would normally produce fish that would return to their stretch of the river. This complaint was compounded by what the fishermen perceived as a further injustice and an outrage: Some of the eggs shipped by way of Portland were delivered to the Clackamas hatchery that propagated the fry for release into the Columbia! The conflict between the upriver fishermen and Hume's canning industry later became the basis for Zane Grey's *Rogue River Feud*.

There are many photographs from the days of the gill-netting industry showing fishermen striking jaunty poses in front of a river bank strewn with huge salmon. We know now that their efforts were too efficient, too successful. In spite of positive input from the Cole Rivers Hatchery on the Rogue, there has been no recovery to the numbers of fish recorded in those days, in part because of the overfishing at that time. In modern times, the salmon runs have been further degraded by the use of pesticides in the Rogue Valley, the impact of logging, toxins from the lumber industry escaping into the watershed, sewage and waste disposal, the commercialization of the river and, of course, the building of dams.

To some extent, these detriments to the health of salmon and the river represent the inevitable problems that arise with growing populations. Before the arrival of the white man, there were never more than 10,000 people living in proximity to the Rogue. Now, there are well over 150,000 people in the central valley alone. But population in itself does not account for all of the problems on the river. Prevailing among those who hunted, fished, mined, and logged along the Rogue, and throughout the American West, was the notion that resources are unlimited, there for the taking in a land so vast they will never run out. This notion has died hard in spite of being a grievous error.

Though his motives may have been suspect, and the practice a less-than-perfect solution, Robert Hume's efforts to restock the Rogue with hatchery fish were an early glimmer in the dawning of a new era on the river and in the nation at large. Environmental impact, conservation, preservation, restoration, and management are concepts that before Hume's time would have left the trapper, the miner, the logger, and the fisherman scratching their heads. Today, most high school students know their meaning and importance.

Rogue gillnetters circa 1915*

Savage Rapids Dam

Where the environment is concerned, as with most human efforts at restitution, it is the most obvious problems that tend to get fixed first. A case in point on the Rogue was the Ament Dam. It was built in 1902, a couple of miles upstream from Grants Pass, by the owners of the Golden Drift Mining Company to ensure enough water during the summer to operate their equipment. To gain local favor, the company also promised that the dam would eventually provide irrigation and power for the Grants Pass region. These promises were never fulfilled, and the dam turned out to be a massive fish killer. In the words of legendary outdoorsman and pioneering river guide, Glen Wooldridge, "That old Ament Dam was a real abortion. The salmon piled up below it and wouldn't go through the dark tunnel of a fishway. It destroyed more salmon than the commercial fishermen ever caught. It just didn't seem wrong to go in there and help yourself to salmon that would eventually die and wash back down to Grants Pass, hang up and stink up the town." "Helping yourself" to salmon immediately below the dam was poaching, a practice Wooldridge and others in the area were not above, particularly in hard times.

The first effort to remove the Ament Dam took place in 1912. Vigilantes, mostly roughneck fishermen who lived upriver of the dam, grew tired of seeing "their" salmon lying below the dam or in a poacher's net. Practicing an early form of eco-terrorism, they blew away a substantial section of the dam with dynamite. There is a certain irony in this, considering that it was the mining industry that had introduced the use of dynamite in the river and tributary streams.

In 1920, not long after the damaged Ament Dam was completely removed, construction began on a second dam a few miles further upstream. Named for the Savage family that lived near rapids that were subsequently flooded by the dam's installation, the Savage Rapids Dam is still standing. It has served the valley well for the purposes of irrigation, while providing the only local water-skiing reservoir. There were problems early on with salmon fry being swept into the irrigation canals, which at times resulted in thousands of young salmon ending up as fertilizer in farmers' fields. Adjustments to the inlets for the water have been made from time to time, which has reduced the problem. Fish ladders, at first very inadequate, have also been improved. Still, there are remaining problems with availability of the ladders to the fish in all seasons because of varying flows. Fish can also have difficulty finding the ladders and occasionally leap out of them onto dry land.

The initial listing of the coastal coho salmon as threatened forced consideration of the removal of Savage Rapids Dam. As of this writing, the dam is scheduled for removal when funding is available. The dialogue over removal has been long and contentious, and the issues too complex to unravel here. There is no doubt that economics has played a lead hand in the final outcome. However, regardless of the motives for removal, when the river returns to its natural, uninterrupted course, fish runs will benefit.

Good news for wildlife along the Rogue, especially the osprey, came with the cessation of the rampant DDT pesticide spraying throughout the Rogue

Valley that took place in the 1950s. We now know that the pesticide softened the shells of the osprey eggs. During the years of DDT use, sightings of osprey were extremely rare and were usually limited to the remote sections of the river. Today, nesting osprey can be seen every half mile or so from Lost Creek Lake all the way to Gold Beach.

We still don't know all the long-term effects of DDT and other pesticides and toxins that have gotten into the Rogue watershed. At times, it seems as though the more we learn, the worse the news gets. However, though it must be considered anecdotal, my observation is that there are far more ducks, geese, osprey, herons, egrets, and other birds along the river than when I was growing up in southern Oregon during the 1950s and early 1960s. This suggests that the river is cleaner, resulting in more for the birds to eat. It could also result in part from the construction of the Lost Creek Dam, which improved bird habitat by preventing the devastating floods that formerly denuded the riverbanks.

Several large salmon runs in recent years indicate that conditions in the river may be improving. However, it is now theorized that these runs are the result of long-term cycles in the ocean's onshore temperature. Unfortunately, these data are hampered by the short span in which accurate temperature recording has been made. Further confounding the issue is the phenomenon of global warming, the causes and devastating impact of which we are just beginning to confront.

The presentation of environmental issues here is necessarily cursory. However, one fact stands out: Today the Rogue presents a poor reflection of its former abundance. If our legacy for future generations is to be something other than remnants and leftovers, we need to acknowledge our responsibility as a society to preserve, protect, and replenish rivers everywhere.

Though the problems are rampant, there are many encouraging signs that the will to protect and restore the Rogue and other rivers is growing. Efforts at restoration on the Rogue in recent years clearly demonstrate that progress can be made when groups and individuals come together in good faith for dialogue and discussion. In celebrating the Rogue, I commend those dedicated to preserving and restoring its vitality. Environmental organizations such as American Rivers, Center for Environmental Equity, Middle Rogue Steelheaders, Nature Conservancy, Northwest Rafters Association, Riverhawks, Rogue Fly Fishers, Sierra Club, Siskiyou Project, WaterWatch of Oregon, and numerous other groups have been working tirelessly along with the Bureau of Land Management and the Fish and Game Commission, and even such large corporations such as Orvis and Boise Cascade, on behalf of the Rogue, its environs, and other streams throughout Oregon.

The many groups and individuals who have dedicated their time, energy, and resources to improve conditions on the Rogue deserve our heartfelt thanks and the thanks of generations to come. Their efforts are founded on, and sustained by, a hopefulness born of the realization that positive change can be made on the Rogue, a living river, still beautiful and restorable to its former abundance.

Cole Rivers Fish Hatchery

THE ROGUE RIVER

Images from the Photographic Journey

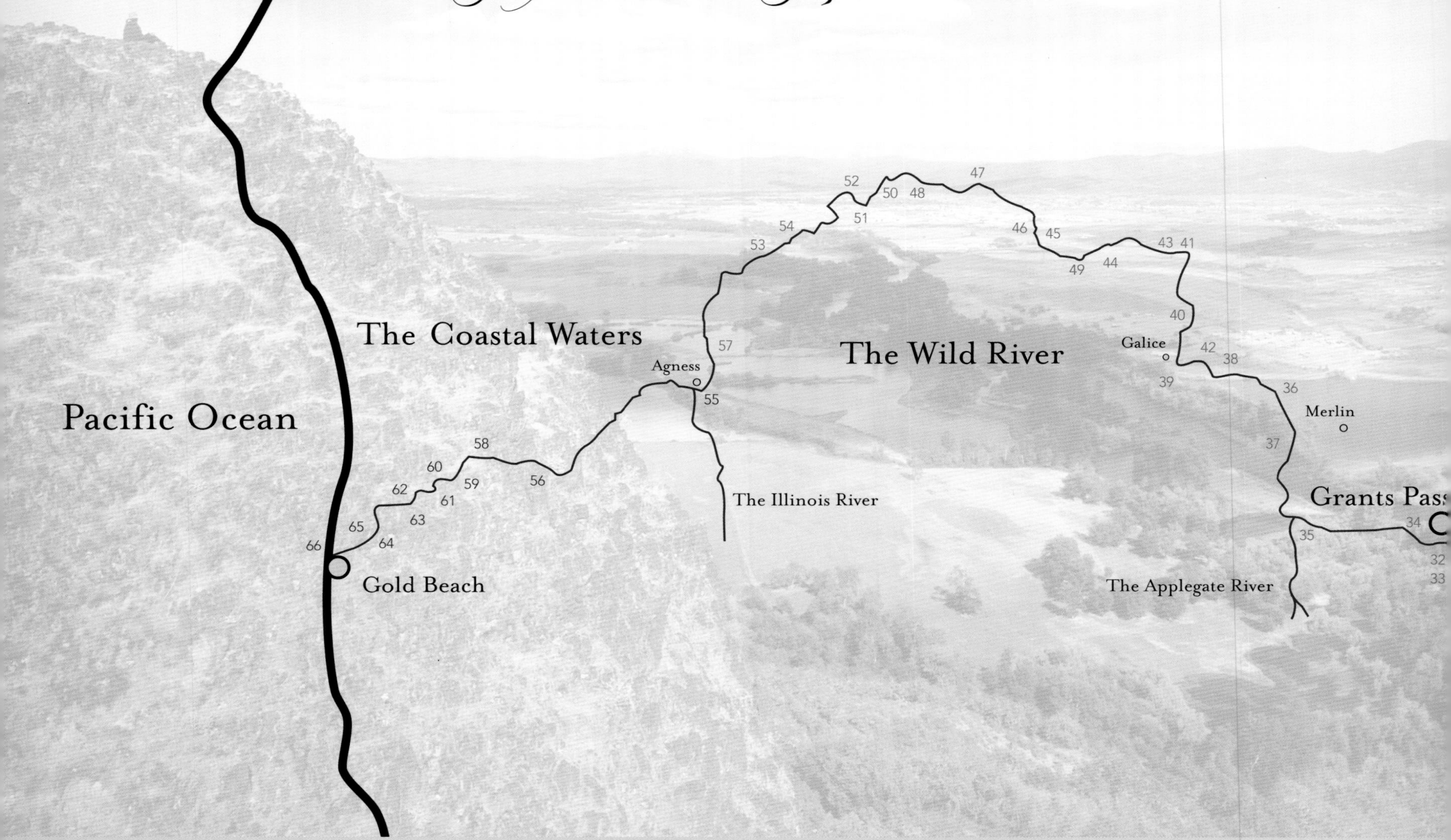

Pacific Ocean
The Coastal Waters
The Wild River
Agness
Galice
Merlin
Grants Pas
Gold Beach
The Illinois River
The Applegate River
52 50 48 47
51
54
53
46 45
49 44
43 41
40
57
42 38
39
55
36
58
60
59
56
37
62
61
63
65
66
64
34
35
32
33

THE HEADWATERS

1. Crater Lake
2. Boundary Springs
3. Alice Falls
4. Ruth Falls
5. Big Bend
6. Meadow Creek
7. Rough Rider Falls
8. Rogue Gorge
9. Abbot Creek
10. Natural Bridge
11. Farewell Bend
12. Below Natural Bridge
13. Takelma Gorge
14. Woodruff Bridge
15. Avenue of the Giant Boulders
16. Mill Creek Falls
17. Barr Creek Falls

THE VALLEY

18. Lost Creek Lake
19. Casey Park
20. Above Shady Cove
21. Dodge Bridge
22. Tou Velle Park
23. Gold Ray Dam
24. Kelly Slough
25. Hardy Riffle
26. Gold Nugget Recreational Area
27. Above Gold Hill
28. Rock Point
29. Valley of the Rogue State Park
30. Hayes Falls
31. Tom Pierce Park
32. Riverside Park
33. Caveman Bridge
34. Gilbert Creek
35. Whitehorse Park
36. Hog Creek Landing
37. Robertson Bridge

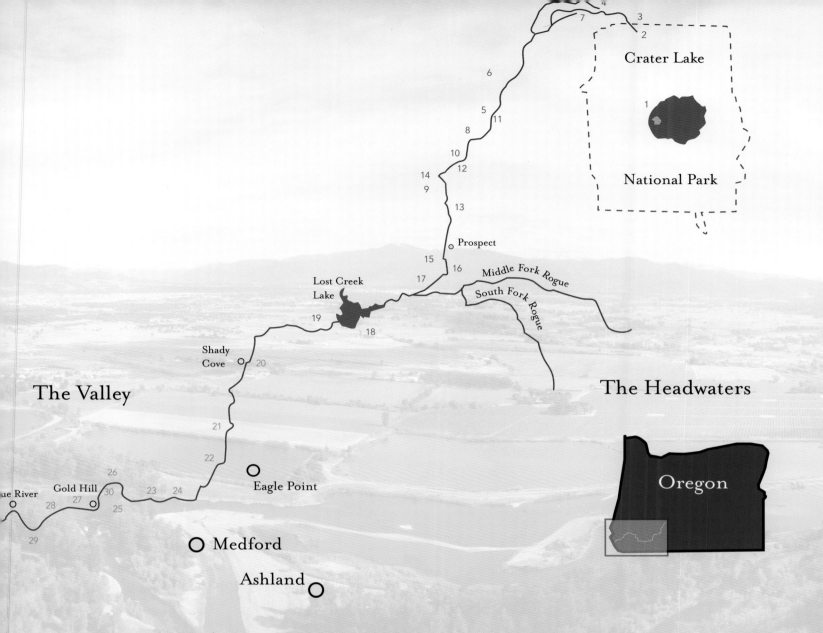

Crater Lake

National Park

Prospect

Middle Fork Rogue

South Fork Rogue

Lost Creek
Lake

The Valley

The Headwaters

Shady
Cove

Eagle Point

Oregon

Rogue River

Gold Hill

Medford

Ashland

The Photographic Journey

THE HEADWATERS

Now has come, an easy time. I let it roll.
There is a lake somewhere
so blue and far nobody owns it.
A wind comes by and a willow listens gracefully.

I hear all this, every summer. I laugh
and cry for every turn of the world,
its terrible cold, innocent spin.
That lake stays blue and free, it goes
on and on.

And I know where it is.

—WILLIAM STAFFORD
Why I Am Happy

OVERLEAF: *Crater Lake*
FAR LEFT: *Crater Lake*
ABOVE: *Below Boundary Springs*

BLUE WATER, WHITE WATER
Discovering Boundary Springs

Water, disguised as a pristine, white snowflake, pirouettes to earth, lighting on jagged, jet-black lava rock 2,000 feet above the bluest water anywhere. The rock is part of the rugged rim of an expansive caldera, a circular opening in the earth's surface five miles in diameter, caused by the collapse of Mount Mazama.

Mazama was a stalwart among the powerful volcanoes of the Cascades that were formed during the past million years. Like Mount St. Helens to the north, Mazama could put on a serene guise, masking its ferocity, sometimes for centuries at a time. Its most active period began half a million years ago when its periodic outbursts shook and reshaped the terrain of the region, while it grew ever taller from the ash, cinders, and pumice accumulating at its peak.

Approximately 7,700 years ago, when Mazama stood at a height of over 12,000 feet, a series of climactic eruptions spread a layer of ash six inches deep over a 5,000-square-mile area and scattered ash across eight states and three Canadian provinces. The eruptions, which were 47 times greater in magnitude than the recent violent eruption of Mount St. Helens, voided the magma chamber deep within Mazama's core, and the top third of the mountain collapsed, forming an enormous bowl where the peak had been. After the eruptions, Mazama continued to belch and spew for a few thousand years before returning to its slumber. Then, calming and cooling allowed rain and melted snow to collect in the bowl we now know as Crater Lake.

There is a depiction of a mountain with a sunken lake at its peak in an ancient Chinese book of wisdom, the *I Ching*. According to the *I Ching's* teachings, this image counsels that "the mind should be kept humble and free, so that it may remain receptive to good advice." The lake is said to convey the attribute of joyousness, while the mountain expresses the notion of keeping still. Together they connote attraction or influence, which may help explain why many people, myself included, have returned to Crater Lake many times to meditate on its silent, blue expanse.

Long before its current popularity among tourists, Crater Lake was known to the Native Americans living in its vicinity. Mount Mazama had philosophic importance for the Klamath Tribe, which considered it a spirit mountain—a place of power, initiation, and vision quest. The shamans of the tribe made the mountain with its hidden lake forbidden to the majority of their people and tried to keep it secret from the white men.

When I was a boy, I wondered where the Rogue River came from and was told that it flows out of the bottom of Crater Lake, a notion that I have always accepted. As folk wisdom often does, this theory has a kind of poetry and beauty, the stuff of myth-making. Imagine a wild river of the Rogue's renown given birth at the bottom of the deepest lake in the United States, a lake of great majesty set like a sapphire in the crown of a mountain. For me, the idea of a river beginning at the bottom of this lake has almost irresistible appeal.

The Rogue's headwaters are over five miles down from the north rim of the lake, at a place called Boundary Springs. There, three converging springs, the largest already a forceful stream, emerge from the mountainside to form the Rogue. Geologists now say that the source of the Rogue is snowmelt that is absorbed by lava rock on the mountain above and percolates downward until it hits an impermeable stratum of clay, which it follows laterally to a point of interface with the side of the mountain, giving rise to the springs.

With this explanation, a river is born but a myth is lost. So which is true? The geologists' theory is made ambiguous by their own admission that water does seep out of the porous lava rock forming the lake basin. Ultimately, the mystery of the Rogue's origin is hidden from view. The explanation you choose is perhaps a matter of temperament. I'm a lake-bottom man. Up on the lake rim, the snowflake doesn't care. In spring, it will join others to melt and be absorbed by the lava rock, or run downhill into the lake or down the mountainside. Whether it finds the tranquility of Crater Lake or goes rushing off shouting "River! River!" it's the same snow and the same mountain; only its fate is different. Blue water, white water.

If you are going to visit Crater Lake, or just traveling through the Rogue River National Forest headed for the high Cascade lakes or the Deschutes River, you may have the opportunity to stop for the night at one of the beautiful campgrounds along Highway 62, which touches the upper Rogue

South Fork

Rogue Gorge

in several places. In the event that you do, your relationship to the river may be permanently changed. There is something revitalizing in the atmosphere near the headwaters of a wild river, a primordial power that can seep into your bones. If a full moon is sending shimmering waves of light skittering across the rushing river while you sit in the shadows of the ancient trees, the river may cast its spell on you. You might return over and over, as I have, until you have experienced all of the Rogue's glory from Boundary Springs down to the Pacific. It is a journey of discovery well worth taking.

Very few ever take the logical first steps of that journey, the relatively easy two and a half-mile hike from the Crater Lake viewpoint on Highway 230 to Boundary Springs. Admittedly, the window of opportunity to make the hike is narrow, since snow usually covers sections of the trail from the end of October until late June. In July, the melt-off is a breeding ground for

Above: Natural Bridge

hoards of mosquitoes. By August, conditions are at their best, but it can be hot in spite of the elevation, and in September and October you must contend with hunters. As a diehard, I have taken the trail during each of the summer months and once in October, when I made plenty of noise so as not to be the recipient of any unsolicited ventilation.

The trail into Boundary Springs is its own reward. It also provides the easiest access I am aware of into a pristine wilderness area. Here is a river at its beginning, completely unfettered and unmolested, without development or dams. Because the river starts small, within Oregon's only national park, it is spared the seasonal parade on other sections of the river: no kayaks, rubber rafts, driftboats, or jets. This proud, boisterous stream, laughing and hollering its way downhill, remains relatively pure and undaunted, flowing on for nearly 60 miles before reaching its first major obstacle, the dam that forms Lost Creek Lake. I have designated the dam as the end of the headwaters and upper Rogue. It is also the beginning of the section I arbitrarily call the Valley, the point at which the impact of humanity begins to weigh heavily on the river.

At its source, the Rogue plunges into terrain that is very young on the geologic time scale. In its current incarnation, the river carves its way through mountains of ash and pumice that form precipitous cliffs, while following and eroding the hardened bed of igneous rock that came down Mazama's flanks as lava during the last eruption. Geologic and topographic evidence far downstream shows irrefutably that a river has flowed out of the high Cascades, generally following the route of today's Rogue, for more than 50,000 years. This tells us that the river was forceful enough to persist, in spite of Mazama's latest upheaval. But beyond the certainty of the river's existence, we have no idea of the route or the look of the headwaters before the eruption. The Rogue's early history on Mount Mazama lies buried in the mountain.

I was full of excitement and anticipation on my first hike into Boundary Springs during mid-June of 1995. The moment seemed symbolic, since I had just begun work on my Rogue River project. After 50 years of getting to know the Rogue, I was finally about to see its source.

Traveling the deep ravine near the trailhead, I got my first close look at the upper reaches of the river. The crystal clarity of the water there is amazing. In places, only the sunlight beaming off the surface confirms that the river is there at all. As I stood contemplating our struggle to restore the nation's many polluted and degraded rivers, the beauty of this unspoiled stream inspired in me a deep sense of reverence and humility.

Beyond the ravine, I hiked the edge of a ridge, teased by the sound of the river below, getting only glimpses until the trail dropped closer for the last half mile to the springs. At one point, still high above the river, I could see it lying in a long, straight corridor of timber. It was bridged by scores of fallen lodgepole pine and mountain hemlock covered with bright green moss and yellow monkey flowers. The crisscross of logs formed intricate geometric patterns that are a predominant feature on the upper Rogue.

Winding River Canyon

Just before the marshy area that signaled my arrival at Boundary Springs, I spied the first waterfall on the Rogue. It is a beautiful double falls that I soon learned is the territory of resident water ouzels. I had just gotten my camera fixed on the tripod and set up on the flat between the two falls when one of the ouzels sitting near the crest of the falls shot off, like a missile, right at my head. The attack was so unanticipated and came with such lightning speed that there was no time to duck or wave the aggressor off. Only the ouzel's sudden upward thrust, just inches from my face, prevented impact. It was a warning. My estimation of its species underwent a quick adjustment. The ouzel is not just a quirky, albeit ordinary-looking, bird with a penchant for foraging in white water with a humorous, rhythmic bob. Its willingness to ward off an intruder many times its size evinced a fierceness and courage born out of a life-and-death struggle for survival in the narrow balance of wild places.

Besides the ouzels, there wasn't a soul around on that first trip into Boundary Springs, but I had a strange feeling that I was being watched. My imagination was fueled by the partially eaten carcass of a deer I found near the trail and what appeared to be a single large canine footprint in the mud at the edge of the stream. The canine print would not have been that unusual were it not for the prohibition of dogs on the trail. A friend reminded me later that there have been no wolves in southern Oregon for many years and suggested instead a feral dog. But feral dogs usually travel in packs, as do coyotes. The single track suggested a lone animal. I have since learned that the area is thought to be habitat for wolverine, although there have been no sightings of the animal or hard evidence found of its presence in recent years. I might have been able to provide that if I had photographed the footprint, which, unfortunately, I did not. On subsequent trips to the site over the next few years, I never had the sensation of being watched again. Whatever the explanation, it lent an extra charge to the thrill of that first visit.

Above the falls, I found myself enveloped in the raging silence of the forest, broken only by the dripping, tinkling gurgle of the snowpack in full meltdown. Here, the young river drained out of a marshy area choked with snags and the nascent bloom of willow and alder brush. Snow patches, dazzling in the midday sun, seemed to float on the surface of the marsh, and all around hundreds of small streams and rivulets were running off the surrounding slopes like liquid light.

I began exploring the perimeter of the marsh, trudging in knee-deep snow that crunched and squeaked under my boots. After about half an hour, I started to tire and feel disoriented. I was sensing a mounting disappointment and frustration because the springs were nowhere in sight when I noticed the small wooden sign with carved block letters. It read simply "Boundary Springs," with an arrow pointing off to the right. It was nailed to a hemlock that still had two feet of snow at its base. The snow also obscured the trail that I assumed was in the direction of the arrow, which on that day seemed to point directly into an area of the marsh where the icy water was several feet deep.

Still determined to find the source that day, I began chasing my tail. I followed the largest runoff stream entering that area of the marsh several hundred yards up the slope to where it fingered out into many smaller streams, all emerging from snow banks and none from the side of the mountain, as my trail guide described. Feeling even more bewildered and

Ouzel at Alice Falls*

tired, I decided that the old trickster, the Rogue, wasn't about to reveal its hiding place on the first visit, so I decided to call it quits and hike out. On my way back to my car, I vowed to return later in the summer after a more thorough review of the directions to the springs.

Boundary Springs

Below Woodruff Bridge

In August of 1995, when there was no snow left at the elevation of the springs, my efforts to find the exact source of the Rogue were not to be denied. After paying my respects to the ouzels, which were still busy at the falls, I easily found the trail around the marsh leading to the springs. Finally, the Rogue at its beginning, and what an auspicious beginning it is! The largest spring bursts out of the red earth amid a jumble of fallen trees and boulders. It is a difficult birth and not picturesque in the traditional sense. The landscape is fractured by the onrush of the determined water, already a stream several feet wide, moving into the light from its subterranean origin. What a wonderful place to contemplate beginning and becoming, especially if you know the Rogue down in the valley, or in the canyons of the Wild River section, or where it meanders near the coast. On that day, I sensed a deepening understanding and appreciation of the Rogue, as though someone close had revealed a long-kept secret from her past.

Crater Lake (1)
Number with caption indicates position on map, page 64–65.

Boundary Springs (2)

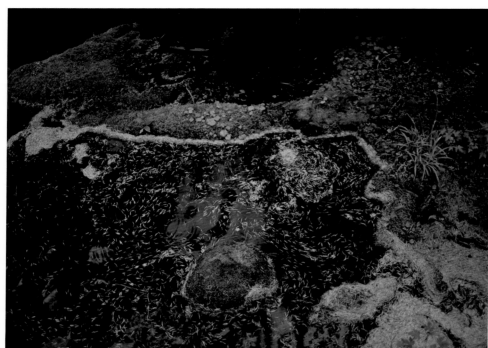

LEFT: *Alice Falls (3)*
BELOW: *Alice Falls (3)*

Below Ruth Falls (4)

Big Bend (5)

Meadow Creek (6)

The river quickened at the turn and spread fan-shaped to circle in at both ends,

running swifter and swifter, narrowing to a glancing chute that ended in a white

roaring rapid. Here was the music of the singing Rogue.

—Z.G

LEFT: *Above Rough Rider Falls* (7)

ABOVE: *Rogue Gorge* (8)

Abbot Creek (9)

Above Natural Bridge (10)

Farewell Bend (11)

Above Natural Bridge (10)

Then suddenly, with a gurgling roar, the river performed a strange antic. It sank underground to reappear far below, bursting from a great dark hole at the head of a gorge and sliding down in glancing green inclines that ended in a silvery cascade.

—Z.G

Above Natural Bridge (10)

Natural Bridge (10)

FAR LEFT: *Below Natural Bridge* (12)
ABOVE: *Takelma Gorge* (13)
LEFT: *Takelma Gorge* (13)

ABOVE: *Near Woodruff Bridge (14)*
RIGHT: *Avenue of the Giant Boulders (15)*

Below Prospect the river tumbled off the mountain in mellow thunderiing music,

...and proud with added strength and beauty, it raced away between its timbered

banks down miles to the sheltered valley...

—Z.G

ABOVE: *Mill Creek Falls (16)*
RIGHT: *Barr Creek Falls (17)*

THE VALLEY

To the ousel, to the water ousel
may it go, may it go.
Tarweed, the corn roots
need this water also.
Buckbrush, the bean leaves
need this water also.
Way of the water's going, we do not wish this!
Let it go to the water ousel,
to the waterskater.
Let the wild goose's wings
carry it upward.
Let the dragonfly larva
carry it downward.
We do not wish this,
we do not desire it,
only the water we borrow
on our way to returning.
We who are doing this
all will be dying.
Way of the water's going,
bear with us in this place now
on your way to returning.

—URSULA K. LEGUIN
Always Coming Home

OVERLEAF: *Tou Velle Park*
LEFT: *Near Casey Park*
ABOVE: *Riverside Park*

TAKE ME TO THE ROGUE RIVER VALLEY
Humanity's Impact on the Rogue

Whenever I read the lines quoted above, I can't help but think of the Rogue River and its "returning." LeGuin's novel, *Always Coming Home*, is set in the Napa Valley of northern California, which is the place that she says she has "loved the longest." Across the tangle of the Siskiyou Mountains, the Napa Valley is less than a day's drive south of the Rogue Valley, the place I've loved the longest.

The poet and naturalist Gary Snyder has called LeGuin's novel "a great teaching story," a tribute to its deep roots in the indigenous soul. I, too, believe we have much to learn from indigenous people, particularly about our relationship to the earth. It is not an overstatement to say that this relationship stands at the core of our prospects for survival as a species. As I began my photographic journey through the Rogue Valley, the rapture I experienced when surrounded by the unspoiled natural beauty of the upper river gave way more and more to the random thoughts of a troubled mind. The visual impact of humanity's presence in the valley caused me to ponder ultimate questions. "We who are doing this all will be dying." And not returning?

LeGuin's poem is used in a place called Chumo by the Kesh, an indigenous people she envisions "who might be going to have lived a long, long time from now." The poem, a Kesh song really, is sung when damming a creek or diverting water to a holding tank for irrigation. The song stands as the finest and most apt invocation I have encountered for those times when we are about to take action that in some way will alter the natural flow of our streams or rivers. Its tone of reverence and humility suggests an ideal standard for our overall relationship with nature. The Takelmas, who inhabited the Rogue Valley for millennia, left us a land intact, with natural resources in abundance. The nearly invisible trace of a house pit, a few chips of obsidian and flint stone—little reminds us of their having been here at all. Like the Kesh, "They owned their valley very lightly, with easy hands. They walked softly here."

There are currently over 150,000 people living in the central Rogue Valley alone and several hundred thousand visitors to the river each year. These numbers contrast sharply with the approximately 10,000 Native Americans living along the entire length of the Rogue before the arrival of white men. At that time, the Rogue Valley was more of a paradise, not just because there were fewer people, but also because of those people's values and way of life. As with rivers throughout America, many of the detriments to the health of the Rogue result from the inevitable problems that arise with growing populations impacting a limited resource. The second factor in the equation is our orientation to the resource. Compared to the indigenous people, we do not own the land "lightly."

I wonder if anyone sang, or prayed, on the day when workers broke ground for the massive Lost Creek Dam? Completed in 1978, with the primary purpose of flood control, the dam also provides some hydroelectric power, irrigation water, recreational use, and control over the level and temperature of the river for the benefit of fish runs—all good things from our perspective. I have arbitrarily designated the dam—this major symbol of our relationship to the land—as the beginning point for the second, very different, section of the river.

From its nearly mile-high beginning at Boundary Springs, the river drops 3,600 feet in the first 46 miles of its journey down to the town of Prospect, not far above the dam. In the next 50 miles that the river travels in the valley, it drops only about another 600 feet. This change in the geographic gradient allows for the warming of the river, which in turn promotes the growth of algae. The impact of this gradient change on water temperature is heightened by the holding of the Rogue's water behind Lost Creek Dam and the other two dams further downstream. An additional factor in raising the river's temperature has been the removal along the river and its tributaries of trees that formerly provided the cooling effect of shade in the summer. Any increase in the river's temperature negatively affects fish runs. Temperature

Lost Creek Lake

increases that go beyond a critical point can result in the massive demise of salmon, such as we witnessed on the Klamath River in 2003.

Along with the algae caused by increased water temperature comes the inevitable influx of pollutants in the populous valley, putting an end to the clarity and purity of the Rogue. Drinking water comes out, and treated sewage goes back in. Irrigation water comes out, and chemicals from fertilizers and pesticides leaching through the ground go back in. Silt goes into the river from tributary streams disturbed by traditional logging practices, and toxins from the impact of our petroleum-based culture find their way in. To experience the impact on the river's water quality, hike the trail into Rough Rider Falls on the upper Rogue. See the amazingly clear water. Put a toe in and feel the icy coldness. As recently as Zane Grey's time, these qualities were not confined to the headwaters. Even when Grey was fishing the middle and lower sections, he mentions the coldness and clarity of the Rogue. The degradation of the Rogue is clearly illustrated by driving from Gold Beach to the bridge over the confluence with the Illinois, a pristine river flowing out of a wilderness area that has virtually no population along its shores. See its crystal-clear, unsullied water entering the murky, green Rogue.

I do not wish to dwell too heavily or exclusively on the troubling aspects of our relationship with the Rogue. I do this as a cautionary measure, while acknowledging that the river brings abundance and joy to the valley. It fosters an economy through the irrigation water it provides for pears, grape vineyards, commercial gardens, and grazing. The beauty of the river and its

Below Tou Velle Park

recreational values are a magnet for tourism. The Rogue's waters are still clean enough to swim in and healthy enough to support salmon and steelhead runs. Locals and tourists picnic and camp on its shores. They enjoy its beauty, the thrill of a jetboat trip, the adventure of paddling a raft through its white water, and the fun of the annual Boatnik. In its democratic way, the river also provides habitat, not just for wildlife but also for people, some living in double-wide trailers and others in million-dollar homes.

As the Rogue flows through the valley, we use it to fulfill our biological and deeper needs, as well. In my old hometown, the municipal water comes out of the river. No newborn comes into the world in the Three Rivers Community Hospital in Grants Pass who isn't bathed in purified Rogue River water. No surgeon scrubs for work there without cleaning his hands in that water, and no cup is offered to slake a patient's thirst that isn't a part of the river's gift. On a deeper emotional level, the Rogue is ever the inspiration for all who come in contact with it, particularly poets, musicians, dancers, writers, painters, and photographers! And no measure can gauge its capacity to revitalize us and bring peace into our stressful lives.

Still, after being able to hike over 50 miles of relatively unbroken trail from Boundary Springs, following the joyous path of a young river, I get a sinking feeling when I see its waters dammed at Lost Creek. I know the dam serves a valuable function. I remember the floods of 1955 and 1964, the terrible devastation and destruction of property. I remember—and I also hear voices. They say, "We do not wish this, we do not desire it." Are they the voices of the residents of Laurelhurst, long gone now, who mourned the loss of their homes and their hardy community that was inundated when the new dam was built? Or could the voices be the river song of another species, the salmon that lost access to their upriver spawning beds? Maybe I am hearing a choir of souls from generations future and past decrying the loss of Cascade Gorge, a deep, narrow canyon with breathtaking views that disappeared when the waters rose up.

*Flooding, Grants Pass 1964**

When we alter the environment, there is frequently a loss for every gain achieved. Lost Creek Dam went in, and the Rogue River lost some of its naturalness and part of its identity. As I contemplate the river's entry into the valley, I feel saddened at the curtailing of its wild, unfettered way. My empathy for it tells me that what falls away at Lost Creek is the river's innocence. Until the Rogue encounters the dam, it is pure and undefiled, a pristine stream playfully finding its way through the mountain terrain. *Webster's New World Dictionary* defines a stream as "a small river" whose characteristic attributes are "moving swiftly," "rushing steadily," and "flowing continuously." These qualities of the upper Rogue come to a halt at Lost Creek. The mountain stream becomes a manmade reservoir.

As the Rogue heads into the valley, it reasserts itself below the dam. It is a little confused at first and partly diverted by the Cole Rivers Fish Hatchery, but soon finds its natural rhythm beyond the concrete retaining walls of the hatchery spillway. Off it goes, bucking and kicking up its heels like a colt that has just been branded and is turned loose to pasture. Looking for awhile like its old self, it begins to widen with the addition of Big Butte Creek, Elk Creek, Trail Creek, and Lewis Creek. By the time it reaches the town of Shady Cove, just 10 miles downstream, the Rogue is a full-fledged river. In its new identity, it rolls on with the strength and maturity of purpose it will need in the valley to withstand the onslaught of human use and abuse of its waters.

With the change to the river, I found the nature of my photographic journey down the Rogue changing as well. I could no longer hike blissfully along unbroken trail, absorbed in the natural beauty. In the valley, there are occasional trails to the river and along it, mostly worn by bank fishermen on their way to a favorite spot. Overall access is limited, though, because of private property. Instead of walking for miles as I did in making the photographs for the headwaters, I found myself driving for hours, sometimes circling back over stretches several times hoping to discover side roads I had missed in my search for new views of the river. Even though three dams make an uninterrupted boating journey through the valley impossible, boating proved to be my best option for gaining a coherent perspective on the river.

I took this option on several occasions. On a hot July afternoon, my wife Patricia and I rented inflatable one-person, orange-colored rafts and rode the rollicksome river from Casey Park down to Shady Cove. It was good fun, we got cooled off, but obviously it was not an occasion for capturing photographs. Once during the early autumn, I hired an outfitter with his driftboat in order to see the 20 miles of river below Shady Cove. I was hoping to get some autumn color shots of that stretch of the river, but was reminded that photography, the way I practice the art, is a solo pursuit. My guide, who had all the best intentions, tried continuously to get us to what he called "the most photogenic spots," which, of course, weren't for me.

A jetboat trip downriver from Grants Pass was all that it is advertised to be—great fun, a chance to see lots of wildlife, even an educational experience thanks to our knowledgeable pilot. The speed and maneuverability of

Jetboat

the large boat provided a thrilling ride, but the frequent 360-degree turns that produced a mild tsunami to cool us off, while successful in doing that, forced me to keep my expensive camera under wraps.

My solo kayaking trip on Kelly Slough above Gold Ray Dam was a completely different outing. Silent, serene, alone, paddling the thin shell in intimate connection with the water, I made several good photographs. Unfortunately, outside of truly still waters, paddling my sea kayak and trying to take photographs along the way caused me the same anxiety about equipment that I experienced in the jetboat. The kayak took on too much water in rapids and was not maneuverable enough in the current. I could go ashore to take pictures, but the kayak was difficult to get in and out of the river in most places. The solution? Driving along the river looking for access.

The result was a reduction and foreshortening of the prolonged periods of reverie that I experienced hiking along the upper Rogue. For the most part, being along the river in the valley is a joy. Certainly, farms with cattle and sheep grazing in their pastures and houses nestled along the banks give the river a very different look than along the tree-lined headwaters. Yet, when I compare the Rogue in my mind's eye with rivers I have seen in the East, where industry abounds and the spire of a smokestack seems to appear on every horizon, it seems to be doing pretty well. Nonetheless, I can't ignore the interruptions to the "way of the water's going." Some of the interruptions are massive, with implications and pros and cons that most of us understand. Others are more subtle, existing in the realm of our consciousness and how that determines the way we relate to the river and its gifts. The extremes of this relationship were most clearly illustrated for me in my encounters with fishermen.

A couple of miles upriver from Shady Cove on Highway 62 is a popular fishing spot called the Highway Hole, where you can practically make a cast from your vehicle. There is ample parking and, although it's a steep scramble down to the water, the rock ledges immediately below are ideal for salmon fishing, if you don't mind plenty of company. When the fish are running, I have seen as many as 25 fishermen in a span of 150 feet of river bank. It's the kind of fishing hole where my father wouldn't have stopped: "Too many fishermen!"

One sparkling spring afternoon at the Highway Hole, trying in vain to look inconspicuous among the fishermen while carrying a large tripod and camera, I approached a fellow who immediately asked the inevitable, "What ya takin' pictures of?" After putting him at ease about my motives, our discourse turned to the fishing. He pointed to a big submerged rock just off shore beyond the ledge that defined the shoreline where we were standing. He cast his lure and dragged it through the eddy behind the rock where he claimed the salmon regularly paused before continuing upstream. He said he had hooked three behind the rock that morning and lost them all, but the day before he had gotten a 25-pounder. The way he described it, catching a salmon there was akin to shooting fish in a barrel. "Ordinarily there's a guy who just camps out on this spot. Only room for one!"

I may have inadvertently met the fellow he was referring to on another occasion at the Highway Hole. I encountered him empty-handed at day's end, just about to get into his pickup. "Do any good?" I asked coyly, knowing he hadn't gotten a fish. He spat a few choice swear words as if to get a bad taste out of his mouth, then told me bluntly that "the fishing has gone to hell! One season back in the late eighties, I caught 39 salmon right from behind that rock down there."

"Wow!" I returned, biting my tongue and masking my distaste with feigned incredulity and admiration. On another occasion I might have said, "Thirty-nine salmon in one season!? You greedy bastard! What were you trying to do, feed the entire town of Shady Cove? Keep only what you can eat right away. Sit down with family and friends. Crack open a bottle of good wine, and before you savor the first mouthful of salmon, thank the fish for its life, thank the river, and thank the powers that be for your good fortune to live where salmon are still surviving. Go fishing after that. Put a couple in the freezer to enjoy during the winter, but turn the rest loose to continue their cycle, and don't turn Highway Hole into Over-Fishing Hole!"

Fortunately, most fishermen on the Rogue are good sportsmen. Some even fish with barbless hooks and advocate strictly "catch and release," a point of view completely absent on the river 50 years ago when "meat fishermen" abounded.

I met the classic antithesis of the "meat fisherman" while photographing at Pierce Riffle, a favorite fishing place of Zane Grey. There I came across a young man of high school age whose salmon rod was bowed nearly into a semi-circle from the weight of a big one he was fighting. He battled the fish for nearly half an hour before one of his buddies netted the large Chinook in the shallows of the gravel bar at the edge of the riffle. With his buddy and another boy oohing and aahing at the size of their friend's catch, he proclaimed, "Can't keep him. Gotta let him go. I snagged him in the back." He was right. By the letter of the law it is illegal to keep a fish not properly hooked in the jaw.

His friends watched quietly in disbelief as the young man carefully worked the hook through the salmon's back where it was embedded just above the dorsal fin and then cut the leader. Having freed it from the hook, he eased the silvery hulk back into the current, where it immediately broke the silence with a mighty slap of its tail, sending out a shower of shimmering droplets that were still falling after it dove and disappeared into the seething green pool below the riffle.

ABOVE: *Highway Hole*
BELOW: *Fish catch circa 1910**

There is only one thing wrong with a fishing day - its staggering brevity. If a man spent all his days fishing, life would seem to be a swift dream.

—Z.G

Lost Creek Lake (18)

Casey Park (19)

Above Shady Cove (20)

Near Dodge Bridge (21)

Tou Velle Park (22)

ABOVE: *Tou Velle Park (22)*
RIGHT: *Below Tou Velle Park (22)*

Who cares? Only, for instance as far as the rivers are concerned, a few sentimental fishermen? But even they should band together to protect so much of vanishing America for their children.

—Z.G

Gold Ray Dam (23)

Gold Ray Dam (23)

Kelly Slough (24)

Hardy Riffle (25)

LEFT: *Gold Nugget Recreational Area* (26)
BELOW: *Above Gold Hill* (27)

Rock Point (28)

LEFT: *Valley of the Rogue State Park (29)*
ABOVE: *Hayes Falls (30)*

Tom Pierce Park (31)

Riverside Park (32)

ABOVE: *Riverside Park (32)*

RIGHT: *View from Caveman Bridge (33)*

... strong with life and immutable to extend it forever, they sought the rolling

Rogue to fulfill their part in the cycle.

—Z.G

FAR LEFT: *Gilbert Creek (34)*
LEFT: *Below Whitehorse Park (35)*
BELOW: *Below Whitehorse Park (35)*

The valley burned gold and purple; clouds melted away in the radiant blue; the mountain slopes seemed bursting in full autumnal glory, the dark green boldly infringed upon by the reds, the scarlets, the cerise and magenta and the dominating splashes of gold.

—Z.G

ABOVE: *Hog Creek Landing (36)*
RIGHT: *Below Robertson Bridge (37)*

THE WILD RIVER

The best thing that we have learned from nearly five hundred years of contact with the American wilderness is restraint, the willingness to hold our hand: to visit such places for our souls' good, but leave no tracks.

—WALLACE STEGNER
Where the Bluebird Sings to
the Lemonade Springs

OVERLEAF: *Blossom Bar*
LEFT: *Hellgate Canyon*
ABOVE: *Hellgate Canyon*

WHO PUT THE WILD IN THE WILD AND SCENIC?
Rafting the Wild and Scenic Section of the Rogue

Where does the wild Rogue River begin? According to the official designation, the Wild and Scenic Rogue begins at Grave Creek. My starting point for the wild river is 12 miles upstream from the official Department of Interior designation. I chose the mouth of Hellgate Canyon not to be contrary, but for compelling visual, geologic, and historical reasons. The massive rock formations and abrupt stone walls of the canyon clearly signify the end of the Rogue Valley and the beginning of the river's journey through the Klamath Mountains. From this point on, for 50 miles the Rogue twists and turns among precipitous peaks. It carves its way through rock thrust up from the earth's core millions of years ago, creating extraterrestrial formations and deep, narrow canyons in stark contrast to the openness of the alluvial floodplain that is the valley.

The movement downstream from smooth and flat to rugged and inclined terrain produces an increase in the speed and turbulence of the river's flow. Although no match for the 3,600-foot plunge from Boundary Springs to Prospect, the gradient increase in the wild section, combined with the ruggedness of the land and increased volume from the addition of the Applegate and many smaller tributaries, creates the largest and most abundant rapids on the Rogue. In this section are found numerous class III and IV rapids and even one class V rapid, Rainie Falls. In the language of this classification system, boaters are cautioned that "imminent death" awaits those who challenge a class V rapid head-on.

The first significant white water below Grants Pass occurs as the river leaves Hellgate Canyon. Though it is well above the official Wild and Scenic Rogue, Dunn Riffle, named after a man who drowned there, has long given pause to boaters. Legendary river guide Glen Wooldridge and his pal Cal Allen "looked it over pretty closely" in 1915 when they made the first documented downriver trip. Later, in 1947, at the end of what he referred to as the "blasting years," Wooldridge dynamited a big rock out of the river there. That "shot" was the furthest upstream that they dynamited in their efforts over time to neutralize rapids that were extremely hazardous or that had to be portaged around because there was no clear channel. It no doubt made passage considerably easier, but in the early 1960s, Dunn Riffle was still the most dangerous point on the river for the hydroplanes participating in the annual Boatnik Race. The rapid seems to have mellowed even more over the years, possibly the result of the 1964 flood, which may have reconfigured the boulders in the river. Rafters and inflatable kayak first-timers now go over it with relative ease. Still, it does have a class II designation, the first white water below Grants Pass to be rated more than a class I.

Because of the changes in the terrain and the character of the river from Hellgate Canyon on down, Hog Creek Landing, just above the entry to the canyon, was called Last Chance Landing. It was given the name by the gill net fishermen who used the place as a takeout during the years of commercial fishing on the Rogue, from roughly 1880 to 1935. During the early years of gillnetting, the crews would put in at Grants Pass and fish through the night. By dawn, they had traveled 15 miles downstream to Hog Creek, where they went ashore and loaded their catch and boats onto wagons drawn by teams of horses or mules, which carried them back to town. Because the mountains went right up from the river below Hog Creek, there were virtually no usable roads or takeouts for the wagons; hence the nickname Last Chance Landing, truly the end of the valley and the beginning of the wild river.

Twenty years after commercial fishing ended on the river, our family would occasionally follow the return route of the early gillnetters. During the 1950s, my father's suggestion of a Sunday afternoon car trip to Hellgate Canyon was a call to adventure to my ears. If he heard that the steelhead were hitting on that section of the river, and if our '42 Plymouth coupe was running well, he would broach the idea on the way home from church with his usual terseness, but with an unusual enthusiasm in his voice that he reserved for just such moments.

"Let's go downriver!" He said it like the idea had just popped into his head.

"Hellgate!?" I returned, more than matching his enthusiasm.

"Yeah!"

"Oh boy!!"

After a quick lunch at home, my father and I scurried around gathering the fishing gear while my mother and sister put together their diversions: knitting, a book to read, my sister's watercolors. As a teenager, I also carried a gold pan along in the hope of "raising some color" if I got bored with fishing. The last item was the canvas water bag that we hung by its rope handle on the front bumper in case the Plymouth overheated, causing the radiator to boil over.

On the secondary roads we traveled, it took about an hour to get to Hellgate Canyon. The last five miles beyond the little mill town of Merlin were gravel road. Between Jump Off Joe Creek and Hog Creek, the road suddenly became rougher and narrower. Where it began the ascent along the rim of the canyon, it was barely wide enough for two cars to pass in opposite directions. It was dusty and very winding, twisting and turning along the top of the cliffside with very little visibility ahead and no guardrail to prevent a 200-foot plunge to the river below. My father used to say that the road engineers had just turned a billy goat loose and followed it. Ostensibly, the road was there to provide access to hunters and fishermen and to the few families living downriver, but mainly it served the logging industry that was very active then in the forest above Taylor Creek and Galice Creek.

During full operation, some of the logging crews would be working on Sundays in an effort to finish cutting an area before the late fall rains set in

Boiler for Alameda Mine circa 1900*

now fell. Their long work week got longer particularly if the
een shut down for part of the summer due to fire danger. Con-
e sometimes encountered a fully loaded logging truck on the
d above the canyon.

from around a corner, a mechanical monster loomed before
loding from its huge tires, its soulless headlight eyes staring
the top of our car, its air brakes bellowing and the gears ham-
fening staccato as the driver downshifted. Terrified, we caught
reath. At that moment, the Plymouth coupe felt like a child's
to meet our maker. My father slammed on the brakes, causing
d a few feet and cant sideways on the loose gravel. Mother's
until the skidding stopped, then, as quickly as she could com-
she announced that she wanted out of the car.

a minute!" The volume and menace in my father's voice hav-
us all, he put the Plymouth in reverse and carefully backed
ot in the road where there was just enough shoulder for the
by. As the red flag on the longest log in the load passed, we all
asp of relief.

that we didn't meet a logging truck, we usually stopped to look
he canyon from the one viewpoint that had been carved out of
se no-nonsense road. The canyon is, after all, the most dra-
cle in the landscape of southern Oregon outside of Crater Lake
cLoughlin. If we had encountered a truck, we skipped the view-

Alameda Mine circa 1906*

point, nervous that another one might be on the way. As we descended the downgrade toward Hellgate Bridge, some of the tension of our encounter was released by joking at mother's expense. "She nearly put her feet through the floorboards that time!"

Full relief didn't come until we got down to the river and across the bridge, which was one-way at the time and still had wooden planking. Because of its age and the way it creaked and groaned when any vehicle crossed, the bridge passage always seemed harrowing. We comforted ourselves with the thought that we were but an ant compared to the weight of fully loaded logging trucks.

On most Sundays, unless it was raining, passersby coming from upriver encountered an apparition on the far end of the bridge. It was Old Buck. We referred to him as a "character," meaning he was outside the norm in appearance and behavior of people we normally encountered. I always wanted to stop and talk to him, but my parents never did. Over the years, I learned from various sources that he was a part-time miner who lived about an hour-long hike over the mountain that rose abruptly on the south side of the river above the bridge. In the manner of many denizens of the Rogue River Canyon, as the Wild and Scenic section is frequently called, he was a loner, a hermit, but not of the dyed-in-the wool clan of that breed. He liked a certain amount of human companionship, which is why he came down to the bridge on Sundays to talk with anyone who might be willing to converse with a stranger who had a long, shaggy, tobacco-stained beard, was clad in a dusty flannel shirt tucked into tattered khaki pants held up by wide suspenders, and wore an old, grease-stained pith helmet.

Old Buck was willing to take anyone who was interested and didn't mind the hike to his cabin, where reportedly his monologue got a little strange

as he described secret Indian treasure that was buried on his
aimed to have found a series of cryptic signs there, leading to
s hid just before being driven from the area during the Rogue
ur. Never mind that the Indians of the area showed no interest
that's where the pith helmet comes in. Wrong continent.
notwithstanding, Old Buck's presence contributed to our
g another realm below Hellgate. It seemed like a time warp,
ent is less locked in the present, the past being present too.
Buck is no longer standing at the end of the bridge, the tail-
gold mining days and sights like the detritus from the last
on the river at Alameda still give rise to this feeling.
now paved all the way to Grave Creek. While the road is less
is not. Many people assume that the official Wild and Scenic
iver is so named because of its wild rapids or the wild terrain
it passes. A close reading of the Wild and Scenic Rivers Act of
at the single characteristic that separates the wild from the sce-
tional categories is roadlessness. In Department of Interior
wild where "it is free of impoundments (read dams) and gen-
only by trails representing vestiges of primitive America."
signations have their use, but that which fills our hearts and
hen we are about to embark on a journey down the Wild and
of the Rogue is not the product of simply thinking, "Oh, now
a roadless area." Neither is it our anticipation of the scenic
ation. We look forward to the scenic in a manner similar to
h we anticipate a meal at a great restaurant. It is satisfying, it is
rich and, unless you're on an exotic eating adventure in the third world, it is
safe. But add the word "wild" to "scenic" and you have another story.

The sense of the wild that we carry within us is juicy and complex. It
comprises hundreds of memories and associations, a melding of language
and experience that reflects a deep ambivalence. We enjoy and even aspire to
the naturalness, spontaneity, and freedom of the wild until it gets out of
control and becomes dangerous. For instance, most of us enjoy looking at
wildlife as long as it doesn't get too wild and decide to have us for dinner!
Similarly, on one hand we express a desire for freedom, spontaneity, naturalness, and joy in cultural mantras such as "wild and free." On the other
hand, we fear the biker who has *Born to be Wild* tattooed on his shoulder.

Places like the Wild and Scenic Rogue elicit a similar ambivalence. Glen
Wooldridge speaks directly of it in the biography about his life, *A River to Run,*
where he recounts his first downriver journey. "We were awfully scared a few
times, but that's good for you as long as you don't get hurt. When you run
one of those really bad rapids and get through it safely, then you have a great
yen to do it again. Sort of like riding a roller-coaster, only much, much
more exciting."

My own ambivalence about rafting the Wild and Scenic Rogue came into
sharp focus near the end of a five-day trip with friends in late September of
2004. Our last night on the river, we camped below Mule Creek Canyon at

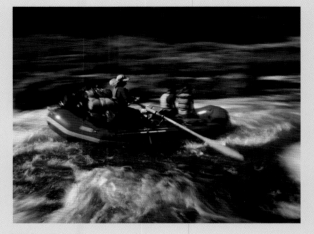

Wildcat Rapids

Tate Creek. It had been a great autumn trip in spite of low water—good company, good fishing and photography, sunshine, the usual thrills and some minor spills. We made it through Blossom Bar, the most technically difficult rapid on the river, with only a little difficulty, relatively speaking. Our gear boat "wrapped" on a rock and swamped, leaving the boatman standing in the water alongside the rock in the middle of the river watching one of his oars float downstream. His wife, who was rowing our paddle boat through the rapid next, dealt swiftly with the situation, getting us close enough to him to pass off our spare oar. Rescue complete!

That night, while we were preparing another gourmet meal, a sheriff's jetboat roared by at top speed in the near dark. We knew that something serious was going on. The next morning before we had finished breaking camp, the sheriff's boat cruised by again, headed downriver. The two men aboard looked grim. Later in the morning, we got the news. A driftboat guide, whose two passengers were fishing, informed us in a hushed, almost reverent manner that someone was missing in the river at Mule Creek Canyon. We later learned that the missing man was a fishing guide. Apparently he momentarily lost control of his boat in the turbulence of a section of the canyon with treacherous whirlpools know as the Coffee Pot, its narrow passage grown even more dangerous because of the low water. The wooden boat struck a rock wall and upended. His two passengers, who were wearing their life jackets, survived. The body of the guide, who was not wearing his life jacket (?!), showed up five days later at Half Moon Bar.

We have no way of knowing the mind of the river guide who drowned or the exact circumstances of the accident. We do know that in the tradition of the best guides on the river, he thought first about the safety of his passengers. We have that from the account of the woman who was trapped without

Argo Falls

an air pocket beneath the overturned boat. Immediately after pulling her out from beneath the boat, the guide disappeared, most likely sucked down by the whirlpools in the Coffee Pot.

The fact of being so close in place and time to a drowning worked on my mind for a full month after our takeout at Foster Bar. At first, I felt relieved that our trip was over and grateful that we had been spared such a tragedy. On the return to Portland, I wondered if, having had my fun and adventure on numerous trips on the river, I should just stick to the Rogue River trail from then on. Later, when I learned the detail of the guide's failure to put on a life jacket in what is acknowledged to be the most treacherous stretch of the river, I came back to my senses. Yes, the river is dangerous. Yes, people occasionally drown in it. But the vast majority of these mishaps involve lapses in judgment or outright carelessness. In the words of Glen Wooldridge,"The Rogue is a wild brawling river and you better respect it."

The inherent risk involved in a downriver trip is mitigated by the fact that the river in its wildness is also very predictable. Although it seems to be a contradiction, the river that we call free-flowing and wild is confined between fixed embankments and for the most part is destined to keep making the same movements around the same rocks year after year. This is especially true now that the Lost Creek Dam prevents the epic floods that formerly moved large boulders around and sometimes changed the course of the river. Except for the effect of occasional high water, which can lodge a tree snag between rocks where you least expect it, such changes now are infinitely slower, produced by flowing water gradually wearing away stone.

In the short term, as evidence of the kind of predictability I am referring to, just watch a single wave, how its curl stays relatively the same hour after hour. It's an obvious fact with important implications. Because of the repetitive behavior of the river, guides know exactly where the "sweet spot" is on every rapid, just as they know which rocks are most likely to be "Tahiti flippers." Guidebooks tell first-timers which rapids they should scout and describe the best route through. Because of the river's predictability, we gain an understanding of, and some control over, its wild nature, which makes our safe passage more possible. Still, the complexity of all the variables, both natural and human, makes each passage over every rapid a unique experience. An important part of respecting the river is developing the boating skills necessary to stay out of trouble.

The kind of merging with the wild that occurs floating a river is a salutary experience that has no equivalent. It is both passive and active, depending on what the river is doing or who's handling the oars. We loll in the still waters between rapids, gliding effortlessly at the river's pace, soaking in the sunshine, the fresh air, and the surrounding beauty. Then, as the muffled rumble of a distant rapid becomes a thunderous roar, we feel the adrenaline begin to flow. We may struggle a bit with the flight-or-fight ambiguity of emotions that are triggered. Our hearts beat faster, our eyes widen. As we slide down the last remaining smooth water and encounter the first wave, time suddenly ceases, and we enter that pure suspended moment where our thinking process is held in abatement while our eyes, instincts, and bodies communicate directly with the river in a struggle for survival.

At least so it seems. Organized raft trips are not really occasions for confronting survival issues. Rafts rowed by experienced guides rarely capsize. If we choose to descend a rapid in the smaller and less stable one-person inflatable, though, all bets are off. Unplanned swims can be disconcerting. On a well-run trip, however, we are taught how to descend a rapid "sans raft," feet downstream, leaning back, letting our life jacket hold us up and the river move us closer to calm water, where there are usually those more fortunate ready to pull us out.

Whether we remain upright in a rapid or take a bath, in that bright moment of descent—however briefly outside of the heavy yoke of time—we are the recipient of a tiny rebirth that gathers with each successive rapid, providing at final takeout the rejuvenation of a river journey. Some speak of the "river high," others of the scales having been lifted from their eyes. Certainly we begin to see and sense more clearly. The scenic is no longer a postcard held up before our eyes. We are inside the postcard, where beauty lives and there is space to move around and enjoy. We are part of nature, we feel more alive, and we discover that there is a deep peace in the wild.

I believe our ever more complex, technological, and urban world creates a longing in us for a more authentic life, one based on the hard-wiring of our species' long hunter-gatherer past, which was linked more closely to nature. A river experience can begin to satisfy that longing. As we allow ourselves to be carried by the motion of the river, we start to find our own natural rhythm, attuning to our original nature, a deep sense of self that is wild and free. In a culture that defines us by what we possess, leaving behind all our stuff to travel down a river fosters the opportunity to discover this connection. Though we are just passing through, for the span of a few days the wild is our home. Walking around with animals, we remember that we, too, are animals. Watching a bear grab a fish from the river's edge or an osprey plunge into the river from 100 feet in the air to snag breakfast for its young, we are moved by their coordination and courage. As we fumble to shelter and feed ourselves along the river, their example is humbling. We are not necessarily better or smarter than they are. If we were there naked and alone, what chance would we have?

The fun, rejuvenation, exhilaration, and connection with nature that most people experience while journeying down the Rogue creates an atmosphere in which former strangers may become friends. Beneath the camaraderie is a deeper connection born of the wild's indifference to our survival. As we sit alone by the river in the failing evening light, the sight of the river dims. Rock shadows make black holes in the luminous surface. The darkened reflections of fir trees creep across the suddenly ominous water. There is a chill in the air. An instinctual emotion built on the bedrock of ancestral memory cautions us that there may be something out there in the darkness. Turning toward the distant campfire, we can make out the shining faces of our companions and hear their faint laughter. Our body relaxes as we move toward them. Imagining ourselves alone there, mostly stripped of that which we have accumulated in life, we discover that we have each other. Our vulnerable condition allows us to see the vulnerability of others, to see ourselves in them. The next day, we take the hand of the stranger we harshly judged back at the parking lot and help him across the slippery rocks.

Argo Canyon

LEFT: *Taylor Creek Gorge (38)*
ABOVE: *Galice Creek (39)*

LEFT: *Rand (40)*
ABOVE: *Rand (40)*

The valley seemed full of supernatural light, a glory too great for land or sea.

... The river, however, took on the most transcendent beauty. It was a living

medium of color, a moving ribbon of rose with rocks of gold reflecting the slopes

and clouds and sky.

—Z.G

Below Grave Creek (41)

Below Ennis Riffle (42)

The water ousel was unaware of me. …it would be wonderful to know all about such a bird. Haunter of rushing clear mountain torrents, mossy-bouldered, fir-shaded, he represented the very soul of all that was alien and aloof to civilization. He was the unattainable in nature.

—Z.G

LEFT: *Below Grave Creek Falls* (43)
ABOVE: *Above Rainie Falls* (44)

A marvelous instinct of nature brought them from out of the ocean depths to the river which had given them birth...when it came it was as if an irresistible command had united them....from then on the progress depended on strength and endurance. They shot the rapids and leaped the falls.

—Z.G

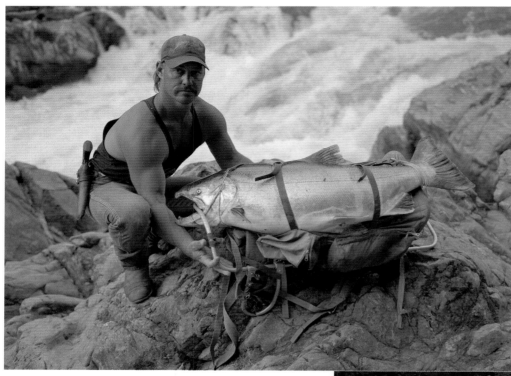

ABOVE: *Rainie Falls (44)*

RIGHT: *Rainie Falls (44)*

FAR RIGHT: *Above Tyee Rapids (45)*

Wildcat Rapids (46)

Meadow Creek (47)

ABOVE: *Missouri Bar (48)*
RIGHT: *China Bar (49)*

ABOVE: *Mule Creek Canyon (50)*
RIGHT: *Stair Creek Falls (51)*

Blossom Bar (52)

Blossom Bar (52)

Through the incredible stillness the low murmur of the river seemed to have a
supernatural significance. That voice could not come only from gliding waters. It
was a gentle and singing sound full of mystery, like the pale-gleaming, starlight -
reflecting water from whence it came... there was something else out
there...Spirit!

—Z.G

LEFT: *Clay Hill* (53)
ABOVE: *Solitude Bar* (54)

THE COASTAL WATERS

*The wild requires that we learn the terrain,
nod to all the plants and animals and birds,
ford the streams and cross the ridges, and tell a
good story when we get back home.*

—GARY SNYDER
The Practice of the Wild

OVERLEAF: *Above Kimball Creek*
LEFT: *Below Coon Rock*
ABOVE: *Foster Bar*

A STORY TO TELL

Whether we have rafted or hiked through the back country or traveled vicariously through the photographs in a book, when we reach Watson Creek, the
official end of the Wild and Scenic section of the Rogue, we notice that the
river makes a great change. Like an old man looking back over a turbulent
youth and a mid-life full of struggle, from here on the river has decided to
take it easy. And who could fault it? With the end point in sight, there is no
need to hurry.

Entering the coastal waters, rapids ebb as the Rogue begins to meander
among verdant foothills, its shoreline graced by bay laurels, red alder, and
big leaf maple. Narrow canyon walls give way to wide gravel bars, and the still
waters of the lonely river become a moving mirror reflecting all that it
passes. My favorite time to photograph this section of the Rogue is late
autumn, when the abundant and varied deciduous trees hold a full palette of
colors, their leaves strewn on the surface of the side pools and estuaries like
brush strokes in an impressionist painting.

In places, the watery reflections reveal that the Rogue is once again witness to the impact of humanity, just as it is in the valley: modern houses and
rustic lodges, an abandoned Ford station wagon, dredging equipment covered with rust, a wood lot strewn with blue plastic, clearcuts and slash burning on a mountainside, pasture land dotted with black Angus cattle, the steel

Lobster Creek

bones of suspension bridges, and a ribbon of black asphalt that shadows the Rogue for 40 miles down to the ocean. What we see reflected in the eye of the river is still primarily a land of great beauty, but one that we have heavily used.

The dearth of activity along the Rogue by November, after the main salmon and steelhead runs are over, creates in me a sense of having nowhere else to go. I am less intense in my search for the next photograph. I let it come to me. The river has a solitary quietness about it that suits the melancholy and contemplative mood of the season. Low clouds float up and down, blurring the tops of the fir trees and hiding the edges of the hills. Fine mist rises from the river like wisps of smoke from a smoldering campfire. It is a time for storytelling.

Lonely, remote areas engender stories as naturally as the leaves fall when summer is over. They seem to be a counter-measure against the all-enveloping silence in such places as the Rogue River Canyon. The devouring cliff walls, the perpetual rush of the river that hypnotically washes thoughts and words from our consciousness, the river's seeming indifference to our lives, and the simple absence of people all move us to assert through stories that we are here, that we matter, that what we did really happened.

It is frequently said that the early settlers in the Rogue River Canyon and the lower Rogue told stories for entertainment, which is certainly true. The tall tales of Hathaway Jones, for instance, are pure entertainment.

One day Hathaway was out hunting and killed a deer. Just as he was approaching the dead deer, he saw two bears rushing toward him from either side. He backed up to see what would happen. The bears began fighting for the meat. One took a swipe at the other; the other did the same. Their fighting continued until one jumped on top of the other; then the second bear did the same. They got to going so fast that they raised up off the ground. Finally the bears disappeared up into the sky. Hathaway said that it rained fur for three days.

HATHAWAY JONES
Tall Tales from Rogue River: The Yarns of Hathaway Jones
(Stephen Dow Beckham, editor)

A good story should entertain, but could have a higher calling as well. It may impart a lesson learned, or not learned, or bear the weight of the teller's desire to be unburdened of grief, guilt, fear, anger, or all four. A good story may be founded on the sharing of sorrow or joy, the telling of a good lie, or the simple recounting of what happened. In the end, the storyteller weaves together the strands of our common humanity, and we are all the richer for the fabric.

Jerry's Flat Road

He waddled off, sniffing for Bunyan, but the white lightning
Hit him between the horns, and he lurched off the trail,
Curling back south to Crater Lake, snorting in the cold.
The sprinkle of rain sifting down on the green country
Thickened, and thunder coughed all across the flat sky,
While the blue ox, plumb lost, on the lookout for Bunyan,
Shoved on, with his ramshackle heart rocking with love.
The tall clouds cracked and it rained like all hickory,
Babe hobbling nowhere in the black mud, and the spray
Spitting off his tail was building into the Rogue River...

LARRY BECKETT
Paul Bunyan

North Bank

Mail Boat, Lobster Creek

When the Tututini and Shasta Costa inhabited these shores, the end of autumn brought the time for celebration and storytelling. After enough salmon had been dried and the berries, camas bulbs, and acorns harvested and stored, there was time for the Native people to give thanks for the bounty of the season and recount the tales that gave meaning to their way of life. We honor them by telling our own Rogue River stories. The Rogue is a generative and inspiring river, with a richer written lore and oral tradition than any river I know of its size. I have been entertained for hours by the stories of others as I have traveled up and down the river. I have told my story and now I am waiting to hear yours.

In the meantime, I decided to ask the river to tell me a story. In my research for this book, I was never able to learn the names that the Native American people used for the Rogue River. I asked several descendants of the Takelma, who said they weren't sure. A Tututini elder told me that his people called the river "Tulhut," which is the Athepascan word for water. His notion was that the people's lives were so entwined with the river that it was like the sky, which they didn't give a proper name to either. I'm sure that now that this book is in print, someone will come forward with the name I was seeking. For now, I am content to let the river have the last word and then take us on down to the sea.

The Voice of the River

Listen my friend, the river said, while I speak from my heart.

Before the people came to me and gave me a name that they could speak, long before then, I was given another name, the one I keep secret to this day. It is the name given to me by the Great Mystery who names all of the rivers, all of the waters, large and small, who are its children as much so as every other living thing. Like the children of the people, we are named for our special qualities and because we carry the Great Mystery's most precious gift, the living spirit found in all the waters on earth.

There is only one among you who knows my secret name, the one I chose to tell in that long, lonely time before the people came, the one who has been with me the longest, the one I love most and who loves me most. Like a mother who before anything else teaches a child to call her name, I told the chosen one my secret name in order to be known and loved in that long, long, lonely time. It may come as no surprise who that chosen one is. It is the salmon whose grandfather, the sea, named it True Finned, Power Tailed, Iron Willed, Current Fighter.

When the salmon child is very young and still with me, I repeat my name at every turn, until the salmon child's world and my name are one. Beginning with a whisper in the melting flakes of frozen snow, I trickle and become a rivulet softly repeating my name. Soon I become a stream running and laughing downhill, shouting my name, dancing from rock to tree, shouting ever louder at each new waterfall. Creek voices join in harmony, and we make a chorus singing my name in every riffle, roaring it in each of my mighty rapids until I reach the sea.

Everywhere, the salmon child hears my name, and in the error of its youth, it thinks that it is me, and I am everything. Content in the ease of its first days, the salmon flows with my current; dear one, so foolish and self-assured, playing until it reaches the sea, which you surely know is the beginning and ending place of all things. With the first sting of salt water in its gills, the salmon child becomes confused and frightened as the sea draws it farther and farther from the sound of my name. "Where am I? Who am I?" it cries, unaware that it has no name and that its days of learning and growing have only just begun.

Jerry's Flat

A name is given to Native children after their elders have seen who they are, and so it is with the salmon, who must grow in strength and understanding for a long time before its grandfather, the sea, speaks in a powerful voice that no one can deny, "You are the one I call True Finned, Power Tailed, Iron Willed, Current Fighter!" The salmon then rejoices. "Finally I have a name! But what is that echo I keep hearing?"

Like the Native child who has wandered from camp and hears his mother calling, "It is I, your mother—come home to me!" the salmon hears me calling when it is far off in the sea. At that moment, years after it has left me, the salmon realizes that it has not been forgotten. Taking courage from its new name, the salmon begins its long journey back to the place that it first heard my name. Other fish living in the sea tell the salmon, "It can't be done! You can't swim up that mighty river!" Even the great sturgeon, who has traveled some of that distance, tells the salmon to give up. "Look at me!" it says. "I'm four times your size, and even I can't swim all the way up the river!"

The salmon doesn't listen to the sturgeon. It hears only my calling as it heads upstream, fighting onward, driven by its longing for me. Shallow places, places deep and dark, huge boulders and sharp snags, steep waterfalls, and turbulent rapids can't hold back the one called True Finned, Power Tailed, Iron Willed, Current Fighter.

Now, because you have listened to my story, I will tell you another deep secret from my heart. Even the mighty salmon couldn't swim up my length were it not for this fact, which is true. You can't see it, you probably can't feel it, but I can make my current flow in both directions. This I do so that those I love and those who love me can come home. When the salmon has come back to me, I say with the love that only a mother can hold, "I have helped you all that I could in your difficult journey, constantly calling to encourage you and all the while pulling you with my love current. Now you have returned to have young of your own, but the journey has taken much of your strength. You are growing old and soon must die. Because I love you so and because you have come home to me, True Finned, Power Tailed, Iron Willed, Current Fighter, I will tell you my final secret to soothe you in your time of dying. You and I are one, and your journey has all been a dream."

Gold Ray Dam

Below Cougar Lane (55)

Above Quosatana Creek (56)

ABOVE: *Above Shasta Costa Riffle* (*57*)
RIGHT: *Lobster Creek* (*58*)

The October days had come, gray at dawn, etching the leaves with hoarfrost,

lifting the clouds of mist, opening to the blue and gold above, windless and still

and solemn, wearing through the long smokey hot afternoons to the gorgeous

effulgence in the sky, and on to dusk, steeped in the melancholy of solitude.

—Z.G

The river sang on, glided on, ever the same, yet ever changing.

—Z.G

Libby Creek (59)

LEFT: *Ferry Hole (60)*
BELOW: *Below Jim Hunt Creek (61)*

North Bank (62)

LEFT: *Jerry's Flat Road (63)*
BELOW: *Near Indian Creek (64)*

The sun was westering low and showed a dull magenta through the pall of smokey

haze. The river seemed a moving medium of rose and lilac, incredible to the eye.

—Z.G

Above Wedderburn (65)

Gold Beach Harbor (66)

Here by the chafing tide and with the squall of fierce sea fowl in his ears, the grand peaks of the Cascades and the canyons with their singing river lured him with strong, sweet power.... It was too big, too restless, too cold and aloof ever to rival the Rogue in his affections.

—Z.G

North Jetty (66)

South Jetty (66)
FOLLOWING PAGES: *Mouth of the Rogue River (66)*

PHOTOGRAPHER'S NOTES

AT THE OUTSET OF THIS PROJECT, I decided to include the river in every photograph. I stuck with this viewpoint, even though in some of the images it is only a small detail, a line of mist or a splash of light, barely discernible, among dark fir trees and deep shadows. In a book purporting to be a "portrait" of a river, this might seem like an obvious strategy—if you have a subject, keep it in view. But there is solid ground for arguing that a river isn't just the water flowing there. Photographer Larry Olsen's beautiful book, *Oregon Rivers*, includes a number of "river" photographs without water in them, showing, for example, how a river has sculpted the landscape far distant from where it presently flows.

Including the river in every image in this book was a way of setting limits for myself. On the other hand, by allowing the river to recede to the background at times, I kept open the possibility of featuring its atmosphere, the geology, the flora and fauna, the human activity and culture in proximity to the river. This roundabout way of depicting a subject from the natural world has numerous historic precedents. My favorite example is the collection of woodcuts entitled *Thirty-six Views of Mount Fuji* by Hokusai, Japanese painter and woodcut master.

In assembling the photographs for this book, which covers the approximately 215 miles of the Rogue's length, I wanted to depict accurately the changing character of the river in a geographically sequential way without leaving out any large sections. I think I have accomplished this more in the manner of an artist than an engineer. In other words, instead of slavishly taking 100 photographs at 2.15-mile intervals, which admittedly could have produced an interesting, but very different book, I let the river tell me its story. Where it droned on repetitively, I snoozed and lost interest. Where it became dramatic and insistent—at Rainie Falls for instance—I took more photographs.

Inevitably, some who pick up this book will feel that I have omitted, downplayed, or overemphasized a particular place or section of the river. We each have our favorite spots that speak to us for highly personal reasons: the riffle where we caught our first steelhead or the bluff overlooking the river where Grandpa's house stood before it was washed away in the flood of '64. For whatever bias there is in a highly personal project such as this, I take full responsibility.

Photographer's notes would be incomplete without a disclaimer. Mine is that I am not a wildlife photographer. I did not stalk or wait for the few birds and animals that can be seen in the photographs. They happened to appear as I was photographing a larger scene. I admire the patience and craft necessary to be a good wildlife photographer, but personally I consider it an invasion of privacy. Photographing humans? That's another matter. We forfeited our rights to privacy long ago with the invention of the telephone and mass marketing.

All the images for this book, with the exception of the black and white snapshots and historical photographs, were made with medium format cameras, either a Bronica 645, a Fuji 6x7, or the camera I now favor, a Mamiya 7. I photographed with a fairly narrow lens range, which excluded a telephoto. Almost all of the images were shot with the camera on my ancient Tiltall tripod.

My preferred film for this project was Fuji's Velvia transparency film. It is my standard for photographing in the soft light of early morning, late afternoon, and evening, or when the skies are overcast. I also made images with a variety of negative films, which gave me more latitude to photograph in the prevailing bright, high-contrast conditions along the Rogue.

From the more than 5,000 frames I shot of the river for this project, I made a working proof at U-develop Darkrooms in Portland of each image that I felt held potential for the book. After a painstaking editing process, I made a final match proof of each of the photographs selected for the book before having the images digitally scanned for printing by iocolor in Seattle. Photoshop software was used sparingly to match the digital output to my proofs and, in places, to soften contrast and bring details out of the dark areas, but never to alter the image drastically.

ACKNOWLEDGMENTS

WITH HUMBLE GRATITUDE, I offer my heartfelt thanks to the following people without whom this book project would not have reached such a satisfying conclusion. Indeed, the project may not have reached a conclusion at all without the love, support, and constant encouragement of two important women in my life.

First, my wife, Dr. Patricia Barnes, from whom I do not remember hearing one discouraging word over the 10 years since I began working on the book. Her support in so many ways, her advice, her enthusiasm, her own love of the Rogue River, and her tolerance of all the sacrifice required by an undertaking of this scope truly make this her book as much as my own. All my love to you, Patricia.

My deep love and thanks also go to my sister, Jean Dorband-Penderock. Although we have lived literally continents apart for nearly four decades since I began following my muse, it has been her constant voice I have heard saying "Yes! You can!" It was her suggestion in 1995 that I do a photographic book on the Rogue. At the other end of the project, her initial editing was essential in shaping and refining the text. Much love to you, Jean, for a good idea and for your love and encouragement over the years.

My special thanks go to Governor John Kitzhaber for taking time from a daunting schedule to write such a beautiful and enthusiastic foreword for this book. I suspect he may have been a creative writing instructor in a former life. His humanity, his deep love and passion for the environment - the Rogue in particular - and his concern for future generations are all on display in his poetic words.

I next wish to thank my gals in Seattle: Nancy Duncan, the production manager, and Karen Schober, the book's designer. Nancy told me at the outset that, like everyone else who makes books, I was "nuts" to take the risk and then said, "It's a risk we all take to put something out in the world that we have poured our souls into." Her enthusiasm for my work, her encouragement, and her expertise in bookmaking were of paramount importance in bringing the book to fruition. Of the numerous critical connections she helped me make, none was as momentous as recommending Karen Schober to design the book. I immediately resonated with the artistry and elegance of Karen's work, then learned that she had canoed the Rogue River, which made choosing her as designer a done deal. After that, I watched in amazement as she edited, arranged, and organized the individual photographs and disparate elements into a beautiful, integrated whole. Thanks, Karen and Nancy.

Thanks for the preparation of the photographs go to several individuals and organizations. I want to thank Al Berreth of U-develop Darkrooms in Portland for maintaining an artist-friendly facility where I did initial work prints of all the images used in the book. I wish to thank Eric McCormack for creating the map for the book, for his editorial assistance and help in the initial scanning of the photographs, and Gary Hawkey of iocolor in Seattle for the pre-press production work. C&C Offset Printing in China deserves final credit for the printing of the book. In particular, I offer my thanks to Charlie Clark at their offices in Portland for his advice and encouragement.

A book like this is not created in a vacuum and so I thank those authors and publishers of all the wonderful books that provided background information and impetus for my own. *Oregon Rivers* by photographer Larry Olson and writer John Daniel acted as a touchstone. Their commitment to rivers and the environment was inspirational.

I thank those authors who granted me permission to quote from their work. I am particularly indebted in this regard to the work of Stephen Dow Beckham. Special thanks also goes to Loren Grey of Zane Grey Incorporated for his enthusiasm for this project and his willingness to grant me permission to quote extensively from his father's books and use photographs from the family archive. Credit also goes to the Southern Oregon Historical Society and the Josephine County Historical Society for letting me browse through their archives and use some of their images in the book.

There is perhaps no greater friend than one willing to read the manuscript of a work in progress. For their readings, their friendship, encouragement and sage advice I wish to thank Ursula K. LeGuin, Hyla Lipsom, Ken Margolis, and Dawn Welch. Editor Nancy Jerrick deserves thanks for putting the final spit polish on the text and formatting it for design. I also wish to thank Dawn Welch and her husband, Steve, Bev Moore and Marshal Dixon of the Rogue Forest Bed and Breakfast and River Company, Curt Duvall of the Oregon Trail Lodge, and Rex and Jackie Elliot for their hospitality.

I want to thank all the boatmen and guides I traveled with on the river: Mel Norrick, Dave Megan, Scott Rion, Dale Mostkoff, Bev Moore, Marshal Dixon and Jim Ritter and the crew of Idaho and Oregon River Journeys. I learned a great deal about the river from each of them.

A hardy handshake goes to old pal and fellow photographer Mark Barnes for accompanying me on numerous Rogue River adventures. Let's keep doin' it! And for all the friends who supported my efforts over the years, my heartfelt thanks.

Finally, it has been a privilege to work with the following businesses and organizations whose early commitment to pre-press purchase of the book helped pay for the printing: Evergreen Federal Bank, Fiberoptic Lighting Inc., Grants Pass Visitors and Convention Bureau, Hellgate Jetboat Excursions, Home Valley Bank, Idaho & Oregon River Journeys, the Middle Rogue Watershed Council, Photo Den, Rogue Forest Bed and Breakfast and River Company, Steve Welch CPA, and Windermere Real Estate Company.

WRITTEN SOURCES

David D. Alt & Donald W. Hyndman. *Roadside Geology*. Missoula, Mont.: Mountain Press Publishing Company, 2000.

Florence Arman, with Glen Wooldridge. *The Rogue: A River to Run*. Grants Pass, Ore.: Wildwood Press, 1982.†

Kay Atwood. *Illahe: The Story of Settlement in the Rogue River Canyon*. Corvallis, Ore.: Oregon State University Press, 2002.

Larry Beckett. *Paul Bunyan*. Portland, Ore.: unpublished manuscript, 1977.†

Stephen Dow Beckham. *Requiem for a People: The Rogue Indians and the Frontiersmen*. Corvallis, Ore.: Oregon State University Press, 1996.†

Stephen Dow Beckham. *Tall Tales From Rogue River: The Yarns of Hathaway Jones*. Corvallis, Ore.: Oregon State University Press, 1974.†

Ellen Morris Bishop & John Elliot Allen. *Hiking Oregon Geology*. Seattle, Wa.: Mountaineer Press Publishing Company, 1997.

Percy Booth. *Until the Last Arrow*. Coos Bay, Ore.: B&B Publishing, 1997.

Percy Booth. *Valley of the Rogues*. Coos Bay, Ore.: B&B Publishing, 1993.

Robin Carey. *North Bank: Claiming a Place on the Rogue*. Corvallis, Ore: Oregon State University Press, 1998.

John Daniel. *Rogue River Journal: A Winter Alone*. Washington, D.C.: Shoemaker & Hoard, 2005.

Gordon B. Dodds. *The Salmon King of Oregon*. Chapel Hill, N.C.: The University of North Carolina Press, 1959.

Lawrence Ferlinghetti and others. *Wild Dreams of a New Beginning*. New York, N.Y.: New Directions, 1988.

Zane Grey. *Tales of Fishes*. Lanham, N.Y.: The Derrydale Press, 2001.

Zane Grey. *Tales of Freshwater Fishing*. Lanham, N.Y.: The Derrydale Press, 2001.†

Zane Grey. *Rogue River Feud.* New York, N.Y.: The Curtis Publishing Company, 1929.†

Zane Grey. *Zane Grey on Fishing.* Guilford, Conn.: The Lyons Press, 2003.

Ursula K. LeGuin. *Always Coming Home.* New York, N.Y.: Harper and Row, 1985.†

Lewis L. McArthur. *Oregon Geographic Names.* Portland, Ore.: Oregon Historical Society Press, 1982.

Gary and Gloria Meier. *Whitewater Mailmen: The Story of the Rogue River Mail Boats.* Bend, Ore.: Maverick Publications, Inc., 1995.

John G. Neihart. *Black Elk Speaks.* Lincoln, Ne.: University of Nebraska Press, 2004.†

Wallace Ohrt. *The Rogue I Remember.* Seattle, Wa.: The Mountaineers Books, 1979.

Larry N. Olson (photographer) and John Daniel. *Oregon Rivers.* Englewood, Co.: Westcliffe Publishers, 1997.

Scott Richmond. *Rogue River Fly Fishing Guide.* Portland, Ore.: Frank Amato Publishing Co., 1999.

Gary Snyder. *The Practice of the Wild.* Washington, D.C.: Shoemaker & Hoard, 1990.†

William Stafford. *An Oregon Message.* New York, N.Y.: Harper and Row, 1987.†

Wallace Stegner. *Where the Bluebird Sings to the Lemonade Springs: Living and Writing in the West.* New York, N.Y.: Random House, Inc., 1992.†

†Quoted with attribution in text

This book is dedicated to my parents, Al and Alice,
who had the good sense to make a home on the Rogue River.

Published by Raven Studios
Printed in China by C&C Offset Printing Co., Ltd.

Cover and interior design: Karen Schober
Map design: Eric McCormack
Production manager: Nancy Duncan
1st Editor: Jean Dorband-Penderock
2nd Editor: Nancy Jerrick

Front-Matter Photographs:
Cover: Above Rainie Falls
Page 1: Winding River Canyon (Upper Rogue)
Pages 2-3: Below Grave Creek
Page 4: Rough Rider Falls
Page 5: Salmon at Gold Ray Dam (top); Below Woodruff Bridge (right)
Page 6: South Fork of Rogue River
Page 7: Mule Creek Canyon
Page 9: Silver Creek
Pages 10-11: Above Savage Rapids Dam

Footnoted Photographs:
Page 26: Life Magazine cover, March 2, 1942; with permission from Getty Images.
Page 45: Jenny is thought to be from one of the Rogue bands of Native Americans.
She was a Jacksonville resident, and is photographed here in a burial robe she made for
herself. Photograph by Peter Britt (circa 1900); with permission from the Southern
Oregon Historical Society.
Page 49: Mary is thought to be from one of the Rogue bands of Native Americans.
The identity of the children is unknown. Photograph by Peter Britt (circa 1900); with
permission from the Southern Oregon Historical Society.
Page 75: This waterfall has no official name. The photographer took the liberty to call it
Alice Falls in memory of his mother, Alice Dorband (1912-1995).
Pages 28 and 33: With permission from Zane Grey Incorporated.
Pages 50 and 135: With permission from the Southern Oregon Historical Society.
Pages 53, 54, 59, 61, 104, 107, and 136: With permission from the Josephine County
Historical Society.

Limited edition chromogenic prints of the photographs in this book, archivally sound and
signed by the photographer, are available. See www.rogueriverimages.com or contact Roger
Dorband at 503-297-0848.

Library of Congress Control Number: 2006927009
ISBN 0-9728609-3-2

Raven Studios
405 NW Brynwood Lane
Portland, Oregon 97229
503-297-0848